Montagu de Pomeroy Webb

The Great Power

Its origin, use, and influence; a brief explanation of the necessity for monetary

reform

Montagu de Pomeroy Webb

The Great Power
Its origin, use, and influence; a brief explanation of the necessity for monetary reform

ISBN/EAN: 9783337295349

Printed in Europe, USA, Canada, Australia, Japan

Cover: Foto ©Suzi / pixelio.de

More available books at **www.hansebooks.com**

THE GREAT POWER:

Its Origin, Use, and Influence.

A BRIEF EXPLANATION OF

THE NECESSITY FOR MONETARY REFORM.

BY

M. DE P. WEBB.

" The two greatest inventions of the human mind are writing and money
—the common language of intelligence, and the common language of
self-interest."—MARQUIS DE ~~MIRABEAU.~~

LONDON:

KEGAN PAUL, TRENCH, TRÜBNER & Co., LTD.

PATERNOSTER HOUSE, CHARING CROSS ROAD

1897

DEDICATED

TO ALL

WHO HAVE THE PROSPERITY OF

THEIR COUNTRY

AT HEART.

PREFACE.

PARADOXICAL as it may sound, money is one of those peculiar subjects which, although continually engaging a large share of men's thoughts, is nevertheless at the same time very widely neglected. Whilst practically every member of civilised society is actively endeavouring to accumulate wealth in some form or another, not one in a thousand troubles about the history, laws, or uses of the wonderful device without which not only would wealth creation be impossible, but civilisation itself would cease to be. The consequences of this neglect in the past have been most serious. Every conceivable method of trickery and fraud has been played on the people—their ignorance of the simplest facts concerning the functions of money rendering them the easy prey of both the governing and money-lending classes. In later times, when sincere efforts were made to lay down some principles regarding the nature and functions of money, owing to the

general lack of information on the subject, the
theory eventually established did but little
credit to the Englishman's usually alert and
practical mind. It, nevertheless, had a very
perceptible influence on the legislation undertaken to improve his monetary system ; and
although both theory and system were defective
and injurious, they were accepted by the great
mass of the people of the United Kingdom
practically without protest or comment. ·More-
over, they are current to this day.

The object of the present work is twofold :—

(1) To draw attention to the inadequacy and
imperfections of the theory of money now
generally received.

(2) To arouse some interest in the consequences to British industries which the continued acceptance of a monetary system based
upon an inadequate and imperfect theory, must
inevitably induce.

In attempting this end the author has endeavoured to set forth his arguments in the most
succinct form, and with only such brief references
to figures as are absolutely necessary to confirm
the truth of his conclusions.   Should the reader
desire to go further into details, he will find
much corroborative evidence in the accounts
of commercial progress that appear in the Press,
in the various Diplomatic and Consular Reports

issued by the Foreign Office, in the Board of
Trade Statistical Abstracts and other Returns,
and in the rapidly increasing crop of currency
publications now springing up on all sides.

Those who labour in far corners of the British
Empire, may sometimes perceive facts that are
not so clearly visible to the many at home. A
residence of some years amongst the industries
of the East has not only enabled the author to
experience the power and utility of a monetary
system other than that employed by Great
Britain, but it has at the same time afforded
him ocular demonstration of the check to
British enterprise, and the loss to British trade,
which has arisen owing solely to the recent
fluctuation in the relative values of gold and
silver. He claims, therefore, to speak with some
authority on the practical side of his subject.

Money is the Great Power : that all admit.
But in the United Kingdom there is another
Great Power, without the aid of which progress
is delayed, and reform indefinitely postponed :
and that Power is the Press. Up to the present
the greater portion of the Press has not shown
much active interest in currency reform, and in
this respect it has doubtless reflected popular
feeling. But Blue Books and statistics are not
popular forms of literature, and it is hardly
to be expected that phenomena which are

only clearly perceptible through such media will attract public attention, except by the aid of the Press. And what better subject could be found for treatment by the British Press than facts and figures in which are involved the prosperity and welfare of the British Empire?

For the ready reference of those who may desire to acquaint themselves with the exact letter of the law regarding the extent of the control over the currency exercised by the Legislature of the United Kingdom, the Coinage Acts of 1870, 1889, and 1891 are added to this work, and will be found in Appendices A, B, and C.

BOMBAY, 22*nd June*, 1897.

CONTENTS

CHAPTER I.

What is money ?—Diversity of opinion on the subject : consequent necessity for investigation—The origin of the value of the precious metals—The influence of gold and silver on the actions of mankind before and after the adoption of the metals as money   .   .   I

CHAPTER II.

The introduction and development of England's silver coins—Early currency abuses—Introduction of gold coins—The monetary difficulties of former days   .   16

CHAPTER III.

Effects of the advance of civilisation on the recognised methods of obtaining gold and silver—Growth of economic ideas in England—A new conception of "wealth"—Influence of the new conception of wealth on currency legislation   .   .   .   31

CHAPTER IV.

The modern theory of money—The generally accepted functions of money—How those functions are considered in England's Currency Laws   .   _   _44

PAGE

CHAPTER V.

The modern theory of money essentially wrong—How money stimulates industry—Civilisation impossible without money—The power of money . . . 55

CHAPTER VI.

The difference between modern and primitive money— Money the Great Purchasing Power—A practical theory of money 67

CHAPTER VII.

The legislation of 1816 examined by the light of a practical theory of money—Effects on internal trade of fluctuations in the purchasing power of money—Effects on international commerce—Conclusions theoretical . 77

CHAPTER VIII.

An application of theory to fact—The recent divergence in the values of gold and silver—Cause of this divergence—Nature of the divergence—Index Numbers— Theoretical consequences of fluctuations in the value of money 92

CHAPTER IX.

Actual results of fluctuations in the value of money on the commerce of the United Kingdom, and on the commerce of certain other nations . . . 112

CHAPTER X.

Actual results on the progress of the United Kingdom of a deficiency in Purchasing Power and Stimulus— Actual results of a more adequate Stimulus on the progress of the United States. . . . 131

PAGE

CHAPTER XI.

Conclusions to be drawn from the foregoing—Monetary reform urgently needed—The true nature of money —The direction in which reform should be made . 147

CHAPTER XII.

Details to be considered in the improvement of England's monetary system—The Currency Department of State —The money of the future 167

APPENDIX A.

THE COINAGE ACT, 1870 183

APPENDIX B.

THE COINAGE ACT OF 1889 200

APPENDIX C.

THE COINAGE ACT OF 1891 203

'. . . . Quid non mortalia pectora cogis
Auri sacra fames? . . . ."

VIRGIL, *Æneid* III.

". . . . Money answereth all things."

Ecclesiastes x. 19.

THE GREAT POWER.

CHAPTER I.

What is money?—Diversity of opinion on the subject—Consequent necessity for investigation—The origin of the value of
the precious metals—The influence of gold and silver on the
actions of mankind before and after the adoption of the
metals as money.

WHAT is money? The question appears
too simple to require a moment's thought.
We all know what money is. We are handling
it every minute of the day either in the form
of coins of bronze, silver or gold; or if not
actually in coins, then in bank notes, cheques,
bills, or some other substitute for coins. Money
is simply the means whereby we get what we
want: or to be perhaps more accurate, money
is the only means whereby we can get practically everything we want. This is a matter of
such common experience that it hardly appears
open to question.

And yet if we turn for a moment to the
conclusions of some of the most eminent

writers on the subject, we shall find a diversity
of opinion so marvellous as to almost shake
our belief in the evidence of our senses.
Although nearly every philosopher from Aris-
totle to Herbert Spencer tacitly admits that
money *is* the means whereby we get what we
want, hardly any two agree exactly as to the
nature and functions of the invention. Some
say that it is simply a medium of exchange ;
others that it is a device created by the State
to measure values. Locke and his followers
considered money to be the most substantial
and desirable form of wealth. Adam Smith
and the modern school of economists, on the
other hand, considering money to be simply
a contrivance for facilitating the operation
of barter, argued that it was the least
desirable form of wealth, even if it could be
considered wealth at all. Whence money
derives its value currency writers even to this
day are unable to agree. John Stuart Mill,
with Bastiat, McCulloch, Ricardo, and other
eminent economists, maintained that it was a
commodity: and that its value, like that of all
other commodities, depended temporarily upon
demand and supply, and permanently, and on
the average, upon cost of production.] Others
contended that money was simply a counter
representative of commodities and services, and
that its value was determined by the number
of counters in circulation—a matter, the regula-

tion of which was in the hands of the State. This last opinion is very generally supported by American writers and by others who have experienced the conveniences of a paper currency. Mr. Alexander del Mar, for instance, argues that value is given to money solely by the law which makes it legal tender, and claiming that most of the authorities, ancient and modern, recognise this fact, calls upon the world to discontinue the use of the precious metals and to henceforth adopt paper.*

Amidst this sea of contention the ordinary reader is very apt to lose sight of the familiar landmarks of common experience, and in consequence, to be stranded amongst the absurdities to which modern economists have reduced the theory of money. Forgetting the old dramatist's description of it as

"... the strength, the sinews of the world,
The health, the soul, the beauty most divine,
... Heaven's physic, life's restorative,"—†

a description to the accuracy of which men's actions to this day fully testify,—some modern writers have been so far seduced by the delusive logic of the economists of the first half of the present century as to treat money solely as a device that enables the unequal exchanges of services, merchandise, &c., between man and man, to be conveniently and expeditiously

* Vide *The Science of Money*, London, 1896.
† THOMAS DEKKER'S *Old Fortunatus.*

adjusted. * If money plays no more important part in the economy of life than of a " machine for doing quickly and commodiously what would be done, though less quickly and commodiously, without it,"† why then have poets in all ages and in all countries sung in praise of its almost illimitable power? Why do many earnest men call it a blessing: and others equally earnest, a curse?

The truth is, the subject has not yet been popularly and practically investigated. Those philosophical writers who have set themselves to elucidate the mystery, have very obviously lost sight of some of the facts of which men of business have every-day experience. Men of business, on the other hand, perceiving that " Money makes the mare go," have rested content in the endeavour to accumulate such gold, silver, or paper wealth as would enable them to obtain all they required. The result has been that the great economists, in tracing money to its origin and in finding the motives that first led to its adoption, have argued that those same motives explain the laws of the complicated invention we are using to-day; whilst men of business, occupied mainly with their efforts to accumulate money, have lost sight of the fact that money is considerably more than "an instrument of purchase." The

* *Vide* Mr. DUNNING MCLEOD'S *Elements of Banking.*
† J. S. MILL.

economists have, in short—to borrow a well-known metaphor—described the steam engine as though it were a tea kettle, and men of business have become so familiar with one kind of engine that they have forgotten to how many uses steam can be, and has been, applied.

It is very necessary, therefore, that the matter should be further investigated, for, as before-mentioned, the neglect so to do has led to the most serious consequences in the past, and may be so doing again. The great majority are in the habit of taking such money as they can get, much as they do the air they breathe, asking nothing about it, and hardly realizing its vital importance. When a resident of the tropics happens to be consumed by a fever that medicine cannot arrest, the doctor will at length probably tell him that the locality in which he is living is an unhealthy one, that there is malaria in the air, and that he must therefore have a change of climate. This may be the truth, although neither eyes nor nose can detect the poison. Similarly in the United Kingdom if business profits are not all that can be desired, and repeated doses of "foreign competition" and "over-production" do not afford a satisfactory solution to the difficulty, it may possibly be to the interest of the suffering merchant to listen to the currency doctors, who say that the money he is using is out of order (although he cannot perceive the fact), and that the only thing that will cure him is a change of financial atmosphere. Some such currency doctor may say, "Go to South America," or "Take a factory in Mexico," or "Transfer your mill to Bombay; that is the only cure." In proof of the healthy condition of the industries of the East, such a doctor may probably refer to Japan and China, where progress is now being made at a pace that, if widely realized, would probably arouse the attention of the great commercial nations of Europe.*

All this may or may not be true. If we reflect that the air is an element of the universe in the origin of which man has had no hand, whereas money is a human device, controlled to this day by human power, there are reasons for believing that the latter is more likely to be out of order than the former. In any case it is hardly wise to entirely neglect all study of that which the majority of the human race are so continuously struggling to possess, and on the acquisition of which civilised existence so largely depends.

What then is money? The late Professor Walker, the eminent American economist, said that "Money *is* as money *does*." Although this observation applies with equal truth to

* Vide Foreign Office Diplomatic and Consular Reports, Nos. 1779, 1786, 1803, 1811, 1824, &c.

every instrument man has devised, it nevertheless serves to direct attention to the necessity
throughout this enquiry of testing theory by
reference to fact—a precaution very generally
omitted by modern economists and currency
writers. Had Jean Baptiste Say, for instance,
tried his theories by such a touchstone he
could never have given assent to so absurd a
dogma as that commodities are purchased with
commodities; nor could Mr. (now Sir) Robert
Giffen have so deceived himself as to believe
that gold and silver remain subject to exactly
the same laws of exchange after they are converted into money, as before: for facts most
emphatically contradict both contentions.* At
the same time, when endeavouring to discover
what money *is*, by a reference to what it *does*,
we cannot be too careful to assure ourselves
that the facts to which we turn are those
of which the world is at this day having experience. It is of no more practical use to
establish a theory which only satisfies a condition of affairs that existed in bygone ages,
than it is to construct one which can only be
turned to account in a Utopia of enlightened
and perfect mortals, such as we are never likely
to see. Yet eminent English economists have
done the former, and almost equally eminent
American writers have advocated the latter,

* *Vide* "A Problem in Money," *Nineteenth Century*,
November, 1889; also, "The Case Against Bimetallism."

to the indescribable confusion of all who are desirous of a clear understanding of the subject. A theory of money to be of any practical value must stand the test of a reference to facts around us at this day—facts not peculiar to one locality or one nation, but facts that are of common experience in every part of the world. To construct such a theory must be our first endeavour.

With these preliminary words of caution in our minds we cannot begin better than by turning to history for information as to the money used in the past, and the views held regarding that money. It is not necessary for our purpose to speculate on the idiosyncrasies of the human animal, which find expression in his propensity to truck and barter, and his inclination for personal ornament; suffice it to say that both peculiarities are facts that we must recognise and take into consideration if we wish to understand our subject. As the desire for personal ornament, and for the "kind of distinction which is obtained by variety or costliness in such ornaments," ranks only second in strength, amongst the majority of the human race, to those other appetites which we possess, in common with all members of the animal creation, we can conclude that when our earliest forefathers first commenced to truck and barter, the objects of their exchanges consisted largely of articles which served to gratify this peculiar desire. Such evidence as we can gather from the condition in which modern discoverers have found the aboriginal inhabitants of Africa, America, and Australia, not only corroborates this conclusion, but at the same time informs us of the nature of those objects which have especially gratified the vanities of primitive man. Peculiar shells, glittering stones, and metals of bright colours, have always been greatly esteemed; but above all, gold and silver are metals to which mankind in all parts of the world have invariably paid unusual consideration. Not only are these metals comparatively rare, but they are of a more splendid appearance than all the others; their beauty is not readily disfigured by rust, and they are practically indestructible by air, fire, or water; they are easily workable, and are consequently as useful as they are beautiful; finally, he who possessed them was always sure of the envy and admiration of his fellow-men. Can we be surprised under these circumstances that gold and silver have always been in universal demand?

Of the actual period when money was first used we have no authentic record. The device was probably known to the Chinese nearly 5000 years ago. It will not be necessary, however, to go back to this remote period, as the object we have in view will be sufficiently served by a brief reference to what has occurred

in more recent times. Trading by the aid of
some metallic go-between was an established
custom long before either gold or silver became
sufficiently abundant to enable them to be
employed as money; yet even in such early
periods the desire for the precious metals for
ornamental and other purposes was sufficiently
powerful to induce men to risk their lives in the
effort to obtain the fascinating gold and silver.
The invasion of the southern shores of Europe
by the Phœnicians, seventeen or eighteen
centuries before the Christian era, was in a
great measure prompted by that thirst for
wealth which found gratification in the acquisition of the more precious metals. The great
value which the desires—vain and otherwise—
of mankind had already given to gold and
silver, received an almost incredible addition
when, for irresistible reasons, practically the
whole world at length decided to make use of
these metals as money. The demand for them,
which before had been measured by the extent
of human vanity, now increased beyond all
bounds. At first the value of the new money
was determined by the strength of the demand
for the precious metals for ornamental purposes :
but as the desire for money gradually out-
stripped this demand, the position was reversed,
and the value of the gold and silver freshly
unearthed was at length determined by the
purchasing power of those metals when con-

verted into money. And so it remains to this
day. Senior, in one of his lectures on the value
of money, observes : " The value of the precious
metals as money must depend ultimately on
their value as materials of jewellery and plate,
since if they were not used as commodities they
could not circulate as money." But Senior is
obviously wrong, for if either metal should
prove more useful, or be more widely sought
for as a commodity than as money, it would
very soon disappear from circulation as coin.
And this is a fact that cannot too strongly be
impressed upon the mind : for it enables us to
clearly perceive that gold and silver, although
in wide demand for ornamental and other
purposes, nevertheless now derive the greater
part of their value from that legislation by the
operation of which their use as money has been
so generally confirmed.

Wherever the institution of money has become thoroughly established, there, those who
possessed sufficient money, have generally been
able by its aid to obtain from their immediate
neighbours such necessaries and luxuries as they
required, and as were considered desirable in
the age and locality in which they lived. When
the money consisted simply of pieces of iron,
tin, or copper, bearing a seal or stamp indicative
of their weight, it was only received by those
who recognised the authority conveyed by the
stamp, or by those who were satisfied of the

commercial value of the iron, tin, or copper as metals. The use of such money was therefore of necessity restricted to certain peoples in certain districts. As soon as silver and gold became sufficiently abundant to be utilised as instruments of commerce and warfare, every government endeavoured to manufacture its money of those more precious metals; for whether the stamp of authority was recognised or not, the silver and gold in themselves commanded the services of practically every people in every part of the world. And as the significance of this fact came to be more widely understood, so the desire for the gold and silver increased. Every man longed for that money the possession of which not only brought him admiration and envy, but at the same time enabled him to obtain whatever his fancy dictated. If he were a merchant he could purchase such articles of commerce as yielded in their sale sufficient profit to enable him to add to the stock of money he already possessed, and to the fame and luxury that generally accompanied wealth of this nature; if he were a monarch he could gratify his various extravagances how and where he liked, even to the extent of buying men who, at the risk of their lives, would attack and seize for him the territories and riches of other monarchs. With such facts in common evidence, can we wonder that people, statesmen, philosophers, and kings

were all agreed that silver and gold were the
most useful and powerful forms of wealth?
And can we be surprised, considering the nature
of semi-civilised man, that all classes who could
do so, joined hands in a selfish and often brutal
struggle to possess themselves of these precious
metals?

The struggle was carried on in a variety of
ways, according to the circumstances of the
moment. At one time it was by pillage and
treachery: at another, by cunning and barbarous
legislation. Just as the thirst for metallic wealth
explains in a large measure the invasion of
Europe by the Phœnicians, so the desire for gold
and silver explains the conquest and plunder
of America by the Spaniards. It is true that
Columbus, when he set forth on his memorable
expedition, thought to find a shorter route to
those East Indies the rich products of which
had for centuries aroused the cupidity of the
people of the West; but the reports he brought
back to the sovereigns of Castile and Arragon
of the mineral wealth of the new lands he had
discovered, although absurdly exaggerated, were
nevertheless productive of most wonderful and
far-reaching results. As the inhabitants of the
West Indies did not appear to be able to defend
themselves, the Council of Castile determined
to take possession of the islands. The pious
purpose of converting the people to Christianity
sanctified the project, but the real and sole

motive was the hope of finding gold. All the other Spanish enterprises in the New World, subsequent to the expedition of Columbus, appear to have been prompted by the same motive. " It was the sacred thirst of gold that carried Oieda, Nicuessa, and Vasco Nunes de Bilboa to the Isthmus of Darien, that carried Cortez to Mexico, and Almagro and Pizarro to Chili and Peru. . . . Every Spaniard who sailed to America expected to find an Eldorado. Fortune, too, did upon this what she has done upon very few other occasions : she realized in some measure the extravagant hopes of her votaries, and in the discovery and conquest of Mexico and Peru . . . she presented them with something not very unlike that profusion of the precious metals which they sought for."*

Although the barbarities and treachery which were characteristic of the military enterprises undertaken by the Spaniards in America, could not, owing to the superior ability of the people to defend themselves, be enacted in Europe, the insatiable greed and disgraceful extravagances of the reigning monarchs led to other courses, whereby it was hoped that the precious metals might be acquired and retained. As these courses were of a nature that seriously affected the coins in every-day use, and as they were productive of consequences that eventually led to the adoption of the monetary system we now

* ADAM SMITH, *Wealth of Nations*, Book iv., chap. vii.

employ, it will be necessary to glance at them somewhat in detail.

In the meantime the two facts that must be carefully noted are :—

(1) That gold and silver have always been in wide demand, and have therefore considerably influenced men's actions, *before* they were utilised as money.

(2) That *after* the general adoption of those metals as legal instruments of commerce and effective aids to warfare, the demand for them became practicably insatiable, and their powers, consequently, all but irresistible.

CHAPTER II.

The introduction and development of England's silver coins—
Early currency abuses—Introduction of gold coins—The
monetary difficulties of former days.

FOR about a thousand years the English
people have been familiar with the use
of silver in their currency. Coins made of this
metal were first introduced by the Saxons in
the ninth century, and were found to be still
current at the time of the Norman Conquest.
Anterior to the Saxon invasion Roman coins of
copper were in circulation, together with certain
brass and iron money manufactured by the early
Britons.* William the Conqueror allowed the
Saxon money to circulate, but, following the
usual custom of conquerors, he issued his own
money, — silver "pennies," — weighing about
eighteen grains,† and of the same size as the
Saxon pennies. The silver pennies issued by
William I. and by the subsequent kings of
England, formed for some centuries the basis
of England's currency system.

* CÆSAR'S *Commentaries*, Book v., chap. x.
† *History of Money in Ancient Countries*, ALEXANDER
DEL MAR.

It will be useful to note here the primitive methods employed in the manufacture of money in those early times. Two wooden blocks were prepared, and in each of these blocks was fixed a die, one to give the impression on the obverse, the other on the reverse of the coin. One of the wooden blocks was fastened to a bench, the other was fitted with a handle. The metal was first divided with shears, laid on the lower block, then heavily struck again and again, until a sufficiently good impression was made. It necessarily followed from the rudeness of the implements employed, that the "pennies" when completed were but very poor coins in comparison with those we are now accustomed to use. Some contained a little more, some a little less than the right quantity of silver; the edges of the pieces were not marked at all, whilst but very few of the coins were exactly round. Yet this primitive method of making money was not improved upon until late in the sixteenth century. It can be readily understood that with coins of such very poor workmanship in circulation, fraud of every description in connection with the currency was not only possible, but was actually of frequent occurrence. Goldsmiths and others used to clip pieces of silver from the pennies and otherwise partially destroy them. The "moneyers" whom the king employed to manufacture his coins, very often themselves surreptitiously issued coins of light weight, and so caused inconvenience and dissatisfaction amongst the people. On other occasions the king himself, when in want of money, would not hesitate to adopt the fraudulent device of reducing the weight of his coins, whilst still continuing to stamp them as before, thus gaining a certain amount of silver at the expense of his subjects. With such practices in vogue, we cannot be surprised that the money of those days was always more or less in a state of confusion. So long as the people could be induced to accept light-weight coins, it is obvious that even if good money were issued by the king it would soon be clipped, or so reduced in weight, as to make it correspond with the worse kind of money current; and with the silver dealers, the moneyers, and the king himself always tampering with the coins, we must expect to find continual currency difficulties. It is well to bear these facts in mind, as they go far to explain much of the legislation afterwards taken in the effort to establish a thoroughly sound monetary system.

We are accustomed at the present day to call the sovereign a " pound," but the original pound sterling was a pound weight of silver. No silver pounds were ever struck, but as twelve silver pennies equalled one shilling, and twenty shillings were considered the equivalent of one pound, we can infer that 240 silver pennies were originally supposed to represent one pound of silver.

There was no regular mint before the reign of Edward II., but the king's "moneyers" were responsible for the weight of the pennies they issued. A couple of instances will serve to show how the coins of the realm fared in the days of the early Norman kings. In the time of Henry I. so great an outcry was raised by the people because of the light pennies foisted upon them, that ninety-four of the king's moneyers were banished from the country, some being deprived of their ears, others of their hands. During the anarchy of Stephen's reign, the pennies issued by the moneyers were not only smaller and lighter, and more carelessly coined, but the barons and bishops made and issued money for themselves. Such incidents enable us to form some conception of the kind of money by aid of which the business of the nation was conducted for three hundred years after the Norman Conquest. It consisted of irregularly-shaped pieces of silver, more or less adulterated, with inscriptions so badly executed as to be almost illegible: and in many instances, of pieces of metal bearing practically no impressions at all.

With such money in common use, we cannot be surprised that the frauds perpetrated by the kings themselves should have been difficult of detection. Even if the king's subjects knew that their rulers were reducing the weights of their coins, they would have been unable

to resist the fraud.   On the continent of Europe
the people were continually robbed in this way
by those in authority.   The kings of France, for
example, openly claimed the right of debasing
their coins at their pleasure ; and where the
barons issued coins on their own account, it was
not unusual for the lord to extract a sum from
his tenants every three years, under the name of
monetagium or *focagium*, in lieu of debasing his
money.*   In England the evil practice of reducing the weight of the silver penny was begun by
Edward I., who in 1300 coined 243 pennies from
that quantity of silver which formerly was only
sufficient for 240 pennies.   Subsequent monarchs
continued the practice, making the penny
smaller and smaller, until in the time of Elizabeth no less than 744 pennies, or 62 shillings,
were coined from the pound of silver.   As the
pound contains twelve ounces, we see that each
ounce of silver was made into five and one-sixth
shillings.   Silver remained at about 5s. 2d. per
ounce from the time of Elizabeth until some
twenty-five years ago.

Although silver was the legal monetary
measure in England from the period of the
Norman Conquest until the beginning of the
present century, it must not be supposed that
gold was unknown in England's monetary
system.   The same Cæsar who invaded Britain
extracted large quantities of gold from the

* *Vide* HALLAM's *Europe during the Middle Ages,* chap ii.

Gauls, and the plunder so obtained led to the
establishment of a regular system of gold
coins at Rome.   Although the Roman currency system perished with the Roman Empire,
many of its traditions as to coinage were preserved at Byzantium, where gold pieces of
various denominations were issued for some
hundreds of years.   These gold pieces were
freely accepted (when they could be obtained)
by the many peoples of mediæval Europe,
whose rulers were at that period unable to
issue other than more or less debased silver
coins.   With the fall of the Byzantine Empire,
however, and the gradual increase of trade that
followed the successful termination of the Cru-
sades, the possibility of reintroducing gold
money arose, and the middle of the thirteenth
century witnessed a very general effort on the
part of the more influential princes to add to
their dignity and power by the issue of gold
coins.   In England Henry III., doubtless
anxious to go with the times, and also not
improbably influenced by a desire to rival the
opulence of his Continental neighbours, issued
in 1257 a gold penny of the weight of two
silver pennies of the time, and ordered it to
be current for twenty silver pennies.   The
exigencies of trade do not appear to have
called for this new coin, and the gold piece
did not have any extensive circulation.   It was
not until 1344 that gold coins were successfully

introduced into the money of England, in which
year appeared Edward III.'s " noble." By this
time an expanding commerce had enabled the
new metal to work its way into the currencies
of France, Spain, Holland, and the German
States: and towards the end of the fourteenth
century practically the whole of Europe were
simultaneously using both gold and silver in
their monetary systems.

We have already had occasion to recall to
mind the insatiable demand for gold and silver,
and the all but irresistible power which the
possession of these metals gave to both king and
subject *as soon as they had been generally utilised
for the manufacture of money.* We have also
noticed in a brief reference to the invasion of
Europe by the Phœnicians, and to the pillage
of America by the Spaniards, certain rude
methods by which the stronger races of mankind augmented such supplies of the precious
metals as the mines of their own lands afforded.
We can now examine the more cunning though
equally indefensible means employed by the
rulers and peoples of Europe to wrest from
each other the metallic spoils they were in
various ways gradually accumulating. We
have remarked that the more crafty of the
people used to clip pieces of metal from the
coins in daily circulation, whilst the kings
themselves, whose extravagances frequently
outran their purses, found a ready way of

augmenting their resources in the arbitrary reduction of the weight of the money with which they paid their debts. The appearance of gold coins in Europe simultaneously with the long-established silver pieces opened the way to another ruse, of which the various rulers were not slow to make use, and which it will be necessary to explain in detail.

The same motives which from the earliest times have induced mankind to work and struggle for the possession of the glittering white silver, applied, but with much additional force, to the more beautiful, fascinating, and rarer yellow metal; and consequently, as soon as gold money became a possibility, every monarch in Europe endeavoured to obtain as much of it as possible, both for his own personal use and gratification, and for the advancement and glorification of his country. When the gold coins were first struck, it became necessary for the king to decide how they should be accepted with regard to the current silver coins: how many pieces of silver should be considered as equivalent to one piece of gold. The matter was doubtless originally decided by a reference to the market rate for the precious metals furnished by the goldsmiths, and also by some consideration of the rate at which gold was being coined by neighbouring governments. The result was very different, however, in different countries. Thus, in 1474, about nine and three-quarter

ounces of silver were considered equivalent to
one ounce of gold in Spain, whilst in Italy
(Florence) a little over ten and a half ounces of
silver were required for the ounce of gold.   In
France the coins were struck so as to make
gold eleven times as valuable as silver; in
Germany the gold was esteemed still higher,
and in England the highest legal value was
given to gold money of any in Europe, one
ounce of it being considered as good as eleven
and three-twentieth ounces of silver.

Let us for a moment examine these figures
in order to fully grasp the result of the
difference in the legal values that the various
sovereigns gave to their respective gold coins.
If one ounce of gold was made by law to pass
as the equivalent of eleven ounces of silver in
France, whilst the ounce of gold was at the
same time legally current for, say, eleven and
a quarter ounces of silver in England, it is very
evident that the goldsmiths of the two countries
could make a very handsome profit by ex-
changing English silver for French gold.   The
English goldsmiths could purchase in France
one ounce of gold for eleven ounces of silver;
this ounce of gold they could exchange for
eleven and a quarter ounces of silver in
England, and so make about a quarter of an
ounce profit on each eleven ounces of silver
they exported to France to purchase gold;
and the French goldsmiths would similarly

make about a quarter of an ounce of silver profit on each ounce of gold they sent over to England wherewith to purchase silver. In consequence of this state of affairs the English goldsmiths would melt down and export England's silver coins, whilst French goldsmiths would at the same time melt down and export the gold coins of France: and in this way France would gradually be denuded of her gold money, and England of her silver.

This is but an example of what was continually occurring all over Europe, from the time of the reintroduction of gold into the coinages of the West until the latter half of the last century.* As soon as this effect of the legal rating upon the international movements of gold was generally perceived, every monarch endeavoured to attract to his own dominions the gold money of his neighbours by rating his own gold coins at a higher value, measured in the current silver money, than that which his rival had established. The general ignorance of the times on all matters relating to the science of money, prevented him from understanding that when he obtained a neighbour's gold in this way, he of necessity lost his own silver. All he realized was the indisputable power of gold and silver money for offensive and defensive military operations, and for the gratification of his own extravagances; and he

* Vide, *passim*, SHAW's *History of Currency*.

accordingly endeavoured to encourage the *importation* of the precious metals by frequently and arbitrarily altering his legal rating of the gold coins, and to check their *exportation* by hanging, drawing, and quartering such merchants as were detected in sending gold or silver out of the country!

From what has been already said it can be gathered that the traders of England, both great and small, must have been considerably hampered owing to the defective condition of the money by aid of which they conducted their transactions. Not only were the coins in general use cut, clipped, debased, and in many instances unrecognisable, but owing to the different legal ratings of the gold pieces simultaneously current in different parts of Europe, at one time the silver money—bad as it was—would all but disappear from circulation; at another, the gold would similarly vanish. Several attempts were made to better the condition of the coins in daily use; very severe laws were promulgated against the clippers and coiners, and at the same time new and full-weight money was freely issued from an improved mill that was set up at the Tower of London. But all to no purpose. As the new machine-made money, although of the best in Europe, was received and paid by Government without distinction from the old hammered coins, it naturally followed that the

new pieces were melted down or exported as
quickly as they were issued. Nobody would
pay a debt with twelve ounces of silver coins if
he found that coins weighing ten ounces would
equally satisfy his creditor. But the politicians
of the day seemed unable to perceive this fact,
and they marvelled that everybody should be
so perverse as to use light money in preference
to good money. Scores of men and women
were hanged for clipping, and the severest
steps taken to induce the public to act with
the Government in their efforts to improve the
country's money, but all in vain. The state of
the coinage passed from bad to worse.

"Happily for England," says Macaulay,
"there were among her rulers some who
clearly perceived that it was not by halters
and branding irons that her decaying industry and commerce could be restored to
health. The state of the currency had during
some time occupied the serious attention of
four eminent men closely connected by public
and private ties. Two of them were politicians
who had never, in the midst of official and
parliamentary business, ceased to love and
honour philosophy; and two were philosophers,
in whom habits of abstruse meditation had not
impaired the homely good sense, without which
even genius is mischievous in politics. Never
had there been an occasion which more urgently
required both practical and speculative abilities;

and never had the world seen the highest
practical and the highest speculative abilities
united in an alliance so close, so harmonious,
and so honourable as that which bound Somers
and Montague to Locke and Newton."

The result of these great men's deliberations
was the celebrated recoinage of 1696. Times
were fixed after which light coins would not be
accepted by Government at their nominal value,
and after which the use of them would be
illegal. The capacity of the mints was multiplied, and the defective money (much of which
was not even one half of its nominal value) was
exchanged for good coins at an expense to the
Government of close upon three millions of
pounds—an appalling figure when we remember
that the ordinary annual revenue of the State
did not at that time exceed two millions. As
coins of light weight were no longer legal
tender, and as the edges of the new pieces were
milled, clipping and counterfeiting received an
immediate check, and consequently one half of
the difficulties that hampered commerce were
for the time removed.

But the other half still remained. The
transfer to and fro, now of the gold coins, now
of the silver pieces, resulting from the different
legal ratings of gold to silver simultaneously
current in different parts of Europe, continued
to inconvenience the people and perplex their
rulers. Owing to the rating of gold to silver

during the earlier portion of the last century being relatively higher in England than on the continent of Europe, foreign gold coins were continually being imported, and England's silver money secretly melted down and exported. Although at this period it was no longer deemed advisable to purposely rate gold to silver so as to draw the more precious metal from abroad, or necessary to prohibit the exportation of gold and silver by barbarous laws such as characterised the administrations of some of the earlier Governments, the difficulty was nevertheless one which for scores of years baffled the abilities of England's most noted financiers. When the fact that the deficiency of silver coins was at length understood to arise from the silver price of gold then current on the Continent, all that our wisest statesmen could suggest was an alteration in the rating of the guinea, so that the legal silver equivalent of England's gold coins might approximate that current abroad for the gold coins of Holland, France, and elsewhere. But the result was never satisfactory, for it was impossible for England to decide upon a legal rating for gold exactly similar to that of *all* foreign governments, for the simple reason that different legal rates were simultaneously current in different parts of Europe.

A way out of the dilemma will doubtless occur to the reader. All that was necessary was for the various States to agree amongst

themselves upon a uniform rate at which they
would make their respective gold coins legally
current. By so doing, the goldsmiths and others
would no longer find it profitable to shift gold
from this country to that in exchange for silver,
and *vice versâ*. Unfortunately, however, at this
period of history, when civilisation had not
reached its present state of development, when
both England and the principal Continental
nations were continually engaged in attempts to
despoil or conquer one another, and when, consequently, international agreements, such as are
common now, were unknown, the possibility
of united action does not appear to have even
suggested itself to the statesmen of Europe.
Another solution had to be found, one in which,
whilst each nation could act for itself, the result
would be such as to prevent the money of one
country being melted down and sent abroad,
owing to the legislation of a rival power.

That such a solution was eventually found
goes without saying. As it will be necessary,
however, to explain the growth of economic ideas
by the influence of which the new currency
legislation found favour in the eyes of Europe,
it will be necessary to devote a separate chapter
to its explanation.

CHAPTER III.

Effects of the advance of civilisation on the recognised methods of obtaining gold and silver—Growth of economic ideas in England—A new conception of "wealth"—Influence of the new conception of wealth on currency legislation.

THE latter half of the last century was marked by an evolution in the views held regarding the nature and functions of money, to which students of currency matters cannot devote too much attention. Up to this time the actions of mankind, both individually and collectively, had been very largely influenced by their desire to obtain silver and gold money; for not only did the possession of this money gratify most powerful vanities, but it carried with it, for this and other reasons before mentioned, an almost irresistible power. We have seen that in rude ages every feeling of humanity was consequently subverted in the national effort to acquire the all-important metals. Weaker races had frequently been cruelly slaughtered or made to slave in the mines at the will of their conquerors. With the advance of civilisation such methods of acquiring metallic wealth were gradually abandoned, and more crafty means adopted. Kings cunningly defrauded their subjects by falsifying the money issued from the mint, whilst the people defrauded each other by clipping the silver or gold coins as they passed from hand to hand. With the increase of knowledge these practices were at length considered dishonourable. The alterations of the legal rating of the gold coins with the express intention of attracting gold from abroad was also given up, and the attention of rulers and ruled directed to what was then considered more legitimate methods of acquiring wealth.

But the belief in the power of gold and silver remained as strong as ever, although an advancing civilisation would not permit its acquisition to be compassed by the fraudulent and often inhuman means employed in earlier ages. The great Locke, towards the end of the seventeenth century, wrote: "All movable goods are of so consumable a nature that the wealth which consists in them cannot be much depended on, and a nation which abounds in them one year may, without any exportation, but merely by their own waste and extravagance, be in great want of them the next. Money, on the contrary, is a steady friend, which, though it may travel about from hand to hand, yet if it can be kept from going out of the country is not very liable to be wasted or consumed." He therefore believed it to be the most solid and substantial part of the movable wealth of a nation, and that to multiply the precious metals ought to be the great object of every government.

This view of money was the one generally accepted in England until the latter end of the last century. It was the popular belief that if a country possessed neither silver nor gold mines within its own boundaries, foreign trade was the means by which it could be most satisfactorily enriched. As gold and silver were the principal forms of wealth (for did not all nations who could do so make their money of these precious metals?), it was argued that any trade which sent more money out of the country than it brought in, was, for this reason, disadvantageous to the country at large. All export trades were consequently favoured and encouraged, because it was thought that payment for the goods exported would eventually be made in money, and gold and silver would accordingly flow into the country. Import trades, on the other hand, unless the goods imported were specially intended for after exportation at a profit, were generally regarded with disfavour, for the payment of gold and silver money was considered a loss to the nation. It will be seen that the inevitable result of these ideas was, that the commerce of the world gradually came to be regarded in the light of a struggle for the precious metals,—

D

a struggle in which no nation that lacked gold or silver mines could grow rich except at the expense of a rival. Thus we find that although it was no longer in accordance with public sentiment to wrest gold and silver from the weak and defenceless by brute force, the precious metals were nevertheless as much esteemed and sought for during the last century as they had ever been before.

In 1776, however, a work appeared which was destined to entirely overthrow the long-established belief that gold and silver were the principal forms of wealth. The condition of development at which civilised Europe had arrived by the middle of the last century was such, that men generally began to interest themselves in many of those social and political problems that had engaged the attention of the great philosophers of ancient Greece. Life was now not only very complex, but in some parts of the world—notably in France—the great mass of the people were undergoing intolerable hardships. The outcome of this condition of affairs was an increasing belief that there must be in nature some great laws or principles regarding the social relations of mankind, the operations of which were not yet understood. Several philosophers in France produced works in which they investigated, amongst other matters, the duties of government, the laws of commerce, and the nature of wealth. In this

last matter they endeavoured to show that
wealth did not consist in gold or silver money,
but rather in those material products of the
earth the profitable exchange of which was the
object of trade. In England this train of thought
had an able exponent in Adam Smith, whose ·
*Inquiry into the Nature and Causes of the Wealth
of Nations* produced a marvellous effect upon
England's commercial and monetary policy.

Smith contended that not only were *all*
the products of the earth wealth, but also
every outcome of human labour. Labour, in
short, he considered to be the main source
of every form of wealth. As for money, he
thought it too ridiculous to go about seriously
to prove that wealth did not consist in money,
or in gold and silver. Nobody required money
for its own sake, he pointed out, but simply for
the sake of what they could purchase with it ;
and although it doubtless formed a part of the
nation's resources, that part was generally a
small, and always an unprofitable one.* A
country's riches, he argued, consisted of the
annual products of its land and labour. Those
products were the real wealth of a nation : and
all that money did was to serve simply as an
instrument that facilitated the exchange and
distribution of this wealth. Money was simply
a utensil manufactured for a special object, just
as pots and pans were utensils manufactured for

* *Wealth of Nations*, Book iv., chap. i.

special ends.   Pots and pans were for cooking
victuals, and money was for "circulating commodities."   For a nation to accumulate money
—a mere instrument—in the belief that it was
hoarding wealth, was as absurd as it would be
for a householder to store up supplies of cooking utensils in the belief that he was thereby
becoming a rich man.*

This new view of money was supported by
a reference to the part played by the device
in primitive societies, where exchanges of commodities must have taken place even before
money was known.   In early times money was
simply a go-between that facilitated exchanges;
and, argued Smith, although trade was more
complicated with civilised races than amongst
primitive peoples, modern commerce was in fact
nothing more than a complex system of barter ;
and modern money, like the commodities first
utilised to facilitate exchanges, continued to
serve simply in the capacity of a go-between,
that enabled business transactions to be adjusted
more quickly and conveniently than they could
be without such a medium.

The effect of these arguments upon English
legislation was very marked.   The restrictions
to the importation of foreign merchandise, which
formerly had been thought desirable in order,
amongst other reasons, to prevent England's
money going abroad, were gradually withdrawn,

* *Wealth of Nations*, Book iv., chap. i.

and finally gold and silver were permitted to be moved in or out of the country according as the circumstances of the moment demanded.   But one of the most notable results of Smith's new doctrines was the success that attended Lord Liverpool's proposal to abandon the silver that had served England as money for nearly a thousand years.

It will be remembered that the currency problems that had up to this time engaged the attention of England's statesmen were two : (1) to maintain in circulation the good, full-weight coins issued from time to time by the mint authorities ; (2) to overcome the serious inconveniences arising from the continual efflux now of the gold coins, now of the silver pieces, induced solely by the dissimilar legal ratings of gold to silver simultaneously current in different parts of Europe.   The first difficulty had been courageously met in 1696 by a great recoinage ; but during the progress of the eighteenth century the money in circulation again became much worn, and in some parts of the country the silver coins had vanished entirely, to the great inconvenience of the poorer classes of the people.

The second difficulty was one which nobody had been able to overcome until Lord Liverpool's "Treatise on the Coins of the Realm" appeared.   In this celebrated letter Lord Liverpool proposed a solution of the problem.   He

suggested that England should use only gold
money as legal tender to an unlimited amount,
and that silver coins should be issued at the dis-
cretion of Government to serve merely as fractions of the gold pieces, and at a nominal value
sufficiently above the market price of silver
to prevent any possibility of the coins being
melted down or exported.

Without entering into an explanation of the
errors that led Lord Liverpool to decide upon
gold rather than silver as the most suitable
metal from which to manufacture the money of
England,* it will suffice to note that his recommendations were, to all intents and purposes,
accepted, and a novel currency system was
put into operation in 1816.† The English
mints were permanently closed to the free
coinage of silver, and gold became the only
recognised money in which payments of any
amount could be legally tendered. As the
silver coins no longer contained the amount of
silver which, as fractions of the sovereign, they
could purchase in the market, no man was compelled to accept more than the equivalent of
two sovereigns in silver money.

The currency system which the law of 1816
established is the one we employ to this day.
None of our coins are legal tender if they fall

* See in this connection *The Silver Pound*, by S. DANA
HORTON.   London, 1887.

† *Vide* Appendix A.   The Coinage Act of 1870 is in sub-
tance the same as the Act of 1816 (56 Geo. III. c. 68).

below the minimum weights specified in the Coinage Act of 1870, and as anybody is empowered by Clause 7 of that Act to break and return to the tenderer any such light-weight gold coins, our money is now maintained in excellent condition. The silver coins of England are current in England for so much above their value as silver that there is no likelihood of their being melted or sent abroad, and the absence of silver money which caused so much trouble last century is now impossible. Moreover, as the Mint is closed to the free coinage of silver, it is no longer profitable to send England's gold money abroad to purchase silver as it was in former times, for silver is now in England, like all the baser metals, simply a commodity.

A plethora of silver money and an absence of gold is also now impossible. In short, the monetary system established in 1816 has been eminently successful in overcoming all the currency difficulties known to financiers up to the beginning of the present century.

There can be no doubt, however, that had Lord Liverpool's suggestion to abandon silver been made in an earlier age, it would have been ridiculed alike by king and people. But at a period when, owing to the spread of the doctrines inaugurated by Adam Smith and developed by other economical writers, mankind were beginning to imbibe the belief that the precious metals were not the most useful or desirable forms of wealth—that they could, in fact, hardly be considered as wealth at all except in their monetary capacities of instruments devised for a special object,—the proposal to abandon one of the metals hitherto utilised as money met with a very different reception. There could be practically no objection to the scheme from the standpoint of the new theory. If the householder found it, for private reasons, inconvenient to use simultaneously both silver and gold pots or pans, what objection could there be to his cooking his victuals in pots of either gold or silver as he preferred? Just as these utensils were made for a special object—cooking victuals —so money was made for a special object— facilitating exchanges. And consequently, if England found it inconvenient to employ simultaneously both gold and silver money to facilitate her exchanges, there could be no sound reason why one of the metals should not be cast aside. Gold money, with the aid of tokens to represent fractions of the gold pieces, would serve to facilitate exchanges in exactly the same way as silver and gold together had done before. The alteration was but an improvement in the device employed to circulate those commodities in which the wealth of the nation actually consisted, and it could not, therefore, affect (except for the better) the accumulation and distribution of that wealth.

Such reflections as these must of necessity
have influenced both rulers and ruled ; indeed,
to this day the great majority of Englishmen
are not only satisfied that money plays the part
of an instrument that facilitates exchanges, but
further, that England's present monetary system
is the best that can be devised for the wants of
the people of the United Kingdom.* To its
success in overcoming the currency difficulties
encountered by our statesmen in the past,
reference has already been made; and we can
be but little surprised that this success attracted
the attention of foreign governments, who were
still experiencing similar difficulties with their
respective currencies ; the more especially as
England's commercial progress during the first
half of the present century was perhaps more
marked than at any previous period of her
history. Under such circumstances it is to be
expected that Continental statesmen would
attribute this progress, in some degree, to the
novel monetary system adopted by England in
1816, as indeed they did ; and in consequence
some of the greatest nations of the Western
world very soon followed in England's footsteps.

Portugal, after repeated efforts to keep both
precious metals in circulation, adopted gold in
1854. Germany followed in 1871-3; about

* *Vide* Sir William Harcourt's reply to the address of certain
of the London Bankers (Gold Standard Defence Association)
of 20th May, 1895.

the same time Holland, Belgium, Sweden, Norway, Denmark, and the United States of America also discarded silver, and decided to establish a one-metal currency with a basis of gold. Although France, Italy, Switzerland, and Greece were not at the moment prepared to admit the soundness of these moves, they closed their mints to silver in 1878, an expedient which India deemed prudent to imitate in 1893. In the meantime Austria-Hungary has established a gold standard, and Russia and Japan * are said to be desirous of following suit at the earliest convenient opportunity.

It has been shown in a former chapter that the greater part of the value of the precious metals is derived from that legislation which confirms their use as money. In face of this fact we should not be surprised to find a material change in their relative values as soon as the leading nations of the world decided to demonetise silver and use only gold as their principal monetary instrument. That such a change has actually occurred is common knowledge. In the eyes of the peoples of the East, gold has increased considerably in value since 1873 : whilst to the nations of the West, silver appears to have correspondingly diminished in value. We shall presently endeavour to trace the results of this alteration in the relative values of the precious metals upon the commerce of the world; but

* Japan has now (March, 1897) decided upon a gold standard.

before approaching this portion of our subject it will be necessary to examine the theory of money propounded by Adam Smith, developed by John Stuart Mill and others, and very generally accepted at the present day. For this is the theory, be it remembered, which, in supporting the proposals made by the first Lord Liverpool for improving England's currency, paved the way towards the establishment of the monetary system we now employ.

CHAPTER IV.

The modern theory of money—The generally accepted functions of money—How those functions are considered in
England's currency laws.

THE theory of money propounded by the
great economists of the latter half of the
eighteenth century, afterwards developed by
Ricardó, McCulloch, and Mill, and finally completed by Bagehot, Jevons, and other modern
writers on currency, is based on the hypothesis
that money, in its essence, is a "medium of
exchange."—an instrument that facilitates those
transactions of life that have always taken place,
and that would continue to take place even if
there were no such a thing as money. That the
invention is very useful in other ways than
in minimising the inconveniences of barter is
universally acknowledged, but that it is
essentially a MEDIUM OF EXCHANGE is the
great fact that Adam Smith succeeded in
bringing home to the minds of the people of
England.

To understand how the modern theory of
money has been constructed, we cannot do
better than picture to ourselves what must have

happened amongst the earliest races of mankind
at that remote period when the device that afterwards became money was originally conceived.
In the first place there could have been no
buying or selling, for the words "buy" and
"sell" imply the offering of, and desire to obtain,
money ; and unless some arrangement were
made whereby men shared labours, each mortal
must have done everything for himself—found
his own food and clothing, built his own house,
and provided his own amusements. The advantages of dividing the work are so obvious, however, that there is no doubt that even when the
human family was in its most primitive condition
some men must have confined themselves to
this kind of toil, and others to that. By so
doing not only would each man become far
more skilful at his own particular work, but
he would be able to get through that work more
quickly, and so would have more leisure in
which to rest and amuse himself. But this
division of labour of necessity involved an
exchange of the products of labour : and as the
human family increased these exchanges must
have been attended with more and more
difficulty. A might not have what B required.
If he did, B might not possess the very article
that A wanted ; so, unless both A and B
happened to desire just what the other wished
to dispose of, no exchange could be made.

Even supposing A and B were both in a

position to supply each other's wants, still there would be some difficulty in deciding, in the absence of any means whereby the relative values of commodities could be ascertained, how much of A's goods should be given in exchange for so much of B's. If A could satisfy B that his hunting knife was worth three goats, whilst B's sack of corn was only worth one goat, it would be easy for both to gauge the relative value of the hunting knife and the sack of corn; but no such method of estimating values would be known in the most primitive conditions of trade. Again, although A might be very badly in want of corn, unless B happened to desire A's spare hunting knife, A might almost starve. Our earliest forefathers must frequently have found themselves in such difficulties before the custom of introducing some intermediate commodity arose.

Here, then, we have the two great inconveniences of a system of barter: trouble and delay in effecting exchanges, and trouble and delay in determining the relative value of the articles exchanged. To the existence of these difficulties economists have traced the origin of money. It must have been early noticed that by bartering the surplus products of individual labour for some one commodity in wide demand, such as corn or cattle, the corn or cattle so obtained, if not required for immediate consumption, could, by reason of its being in such wide demand to support life, &c., be afterwards easily rebartered for whatever object might then be desired. In this way the introduction of an intermediate commodity not only facilitated exchanges, but, as the custom developed, the go-between commodity in itself formed a convenient article to which to refer in order to determine the relative value of other commodities. Thus we are told that the armour of Diomede was worth nine oxen, but that of Glaucus a hundred,—a statement that shows that the early Greeks used sometimes to measure values in oxen.* If the intermediate commodity, besides being in wide demand, could also be kept for some period without loss, it offered a further advantage; for not only could its possessor then defer the rebarter of it until such time as he desired, but he could place it on one side as a store upon which he could have recourse in time of need. It is obvious that any commodity that would keep, and that was in wide demand, would answer as well as corn and cattle; in fact, the longer it would keep, and the wider it was in demand, the more suitable it would be as an aid to commerce,

* HOMER'S *Iliad*, Book vi. In Ounamartch (one of the Aleutian Islands) Reclus mentions that it was customary to similarly measure values in human beings. Thus foxes, sables, &c., were said to be worth "so many women." *Primitive Folk*.

and as a reserve upon which to rely in case
of emergency. For this reason iron and
copper would be more suitable than sugar,
salt, dates, or shells, all of which have been
actually used ; and for the same reason gold
and silver would prove even more acceptable
than either iron or copper.

The above brief outline of the difficulties
incident to a system of barter, and of the
advantages arising from the introduction to
that system of some durable go - between,
affords the foundation upon which the modern
theory of money has been based. Whatever
commodity was used as the aid to commerce,
whether it was corn, cattle, shells, or metal, it
obviously served three distinct ends : it facilitated barter, it afforded a convenient standard
by which to determine the relative value of
commodities generally, and it supplied traders
with a means of storing up their surplus
wealth. Therefore, say the economists : Money
is (1) a medium of exchange ; (2) a common
measure of value ; and (3) a store of value.

Of the accuracy of these conclusions there
at first appears to be no question. The man
who to-day sells his labour for a money wage,
cannot eat or drink that money. The money
is merely a convenient medium whereby he
exchanges the outcome of his mechanical or
mental abilities for such commodities as are
necessary to support his life. The labours of

every civilized community are so divided that the maximum of efficiency and the maximum of production are obtained with the minimum expenditure of energy. Men individually and collectively direct their efforts to the cultivation of special skill at one class of work, and then the various products of their several labours are readily exchanged by the aid of money. But no individual requires money— the medium—for its own sake; it is desired, to repeat Smith's words, solely for the sake of what can be obtained in exchange for it. The part money plays is, therefore, that of an intermediary,—a go-between, an instrument, the special function of which is to facilitate exchanges that would have to be made, although with considerable difficulty, even if there were no helping medium. Such is the argument now generally accepted.

The money of to-day continues to serve as a store of wealth also, just as the primitive media first introduced to facilitate trade so served. Although we no longer consider it necessary to bury our gold and silver in the earth after the fashion of our early forefathers, in handing our surplus coins to our bankers or to others engaged in undertakings in which we ourselves are not actually concerned, we are deriving a similar advantage: we are placing aside a reserve or store of wealth upon which we can depend, and of which we can hereafter

make use, as we may feel disposed. The difference between the way in which we now
store our accumulated wealth, and that cus-
tomarily adopted by mankind in more primitive states of society, is one that arises partly
from the new and profitable uses to which it
has been found money can be turned, and
partly from the additional security which a
more advanced civilisation affords. The fact
remains, however, that the invention of money
provided in the beginning, and continues to
provide to this day, a very convenient means
whereby we can store those reserves of wealth
upon which we do not immediately need to
draw.

That money is a common measure of value)
is also as true now as it was when the device
was first instituted; indeed, in this measuring
capacity we recognise an even more important
function than that of a "store of value." The
one and only method that we employ to
determine the relative values of rights, services,
and commodities, is a reference to their values
expressed in money. We measure everything,
in short, by applying to it the one established
standard—the sovereign, dollar, rupee, or other
coin,—according to the land in which we live. If
we incur an obligation which we do not intend
to adjust until some future date, we invariably
measure that obligation in money. If we wish
to venture upon any undertaking either great

or small, at the moment or in the future, we have only one method of gauging the probable result of the venture : and that is by measuring every detail in money. And this long-established habit of so measuring all things has been confirmed by law. Clause 6 of the English Coinage Act (33 Victoria, c. 10) says : " Every contract, sale, payment, bill, note, instrument, and security for money, and every transaction, dealing, matter, and thing whatever relating to money, or involving the payment of or the liability to pay any money, which is made, executed, or entered into, done or had, shall be made, executed, entered into, done and had according to the coins which are current and legal tender in pursuance of this Act, *and not otherwise*, unless the same be made, executed, entered into, done or had, according to the currency of some British possession or some foreign State."*

With both law and custom in complete agreement, there can be no question that money plays the part of a common measure of value.

At this point it becomes necessary to direct attention to the first peculiarity with regard to the national treatment of money. Money is admittedly (1) a medium of exchange, (2) a common measure of value, and (3) a store of value. Although this view of the contrivance

* *Vide* Appendix A.

is one that has now universally commended itself alike to statesmen and philosophers, kings and people, and although the manufacture of money has been invariably claimed as one of the prerogatives of the ruling authority, it has never been recognised as a duty of Government to provide for the nation other than an acceptable MEDIUM OF EXCHANGE. The currency legislation of recent times has only had one object, viz., to maintain in circulation well-executed coins of certain established weights, or well-executed paper promises to pay such coins. But no special effort on the part of the legislature has been made to provide the people of England with either a satisfactory STORE OF VALUE, or an equable MEASURE OF VALUE. Certainly in adopting gold and silver as money, modern Governments have incidentally legalised two most suitable metals as stores of value, for not only are gold and silver to all intents and purposes indestructible, but they are at the same time in universal demand. But the necessity of an unchangeable measure of value is nowadays of even more importance than that of a reserve or store of value ; yet, remarkable to say, this necessity is one that has been very generally overlooked. On the one or two occasions when the efforts of the few have momentarily directed public attention to the subject, there have not been wanting those who have argued that the measuring function of money is a matter over which it was impossible in the nature of things for human power to exercise any control. And so the agriculturist whose products are measured by the money he can obtain for them, might find his labours doubled and himself ruined by an unexpected fluctuation in the money by which he measures the details of his business. The manufacturer, whose calculations are rewarded by the profits he can make on the goods he sells, might also find himself in a like difficulty owing to a similarly unlooked-for change in the standard measure of value provided by Government; and so on with every individual in the country. Those Englishmen whose enterprise and industry have led them to labour in parts of the empire where their efforts are measured in silver money, have in recent years experienced a very painful reminder of their neglect to study this measuring function of the great "medium of exchange." And Englishmen at home are similarly dupes of their own indifference to matters relating to the currency, although the results are slower to show themselves and far more difficult of detection.

But the most remarkable peculiarity in connection with the national treatment of money to which it is necessary to direct attention is not the neglect by Government of any methodical attempt to control those two functions of money, which are admitted

on all sides to be of paramount importance
to every member of the community, but
the extraordinary perversion of fact which,
inaugurated by Adam Smith and defended by
the marvellous logic of Mill, has led the people
of to-day to accept as true a theory that has
for its basis so obviously defective an hypothesis
as that the complex monetary device we now
employ is merely a "medium of exchange."
For this hypothesis, to which every attention
has been paid, and to the acceptance of
which can be traced the acquiescence that
followed Lord Liverpool's proposal to dis-
member England's currency, will not for one
moment bear the test of a reference to either
law or practice.   In short, that which we shall
now find to be false has been widely received
as an axiom, whilst that which all have agreed
to be true has been entirely ignored !   It will
presently be useful to trace the results upon
English commerce of this deplorable disregard
of the lessons conveyed by fact and theory ; but
before so doing it will be advisable to consider
more fully what money actually *does*.   In this
way we shall be able to perceive the utter
inadequacy of the current "medium of exchange" theory, and at the same time to gather
some idea of the restrictive and baneful
influence that this theory has exercised upon
the progress of the people of Great Britain.

CHAPTER V.

The modern theory of money essentially wrong—How money
stimulates industry—Civilisation impossible without money
—The power of money.

THE brief reference already made to the
inconveniences inseparable from a system
of barter, and to the parts played by the
go - between commodities first introduced to
lessen these inconveniences, is sufficient to
show that such intermediaries undoubtedly
served primarily as " media of exchange." But
is this fact in itself an adequate ground for
concluding that money continues to serve a
similar end in the economy of modern civilised
life? The complex systems of currency now
legally established, bear but very little resem-
blance to the embryonic monetary contrivances
first employed to reduce the difficulties of barter;
and in its development may not the invention
have acquired functions altogether unknown to
early man? The world of to-day must be so
very different from the world of that pre-
historic period when the idea of money was
first conceived, that we can hardly expect to
find what was true of the device in its most

primitive forms to be equally true of the vast
and intricate machinery by the aid of which
modern international commerce is kept in
motion, and the innumerable complexities of
a highly-civilised state of society are so readily
overcome.

When we speak of money being a " medium
of exchange," or " an instrument that facilitates
exchanges," we imply the existence of a condition of affairs in which certain things are not
only ready and waiting to be exchanged, but
in which those things would be exchanged even
if there were no money. Now, if we turn to
history to discover what things have actually
been exchanged between those to whom the
device was unknown, we find ourselves back
amongst primitive folk, whose trade—if their
petty barterings can be so called—never advanced far beyond the interchange of such
ornaments and articles of rude clothing as
gratified their respective vanities. We find
that until money had been introduced and
generally adopted, the human family have
invariably remained in that semi-barbarous,
agricultural, or pastoral state in which we still
find petty tribes in the far interiors of Asia
and Africa. Search where we may we shall
not be able to discover one solitary example
of a marked advance in the direction of social
unity, political progress, and civilisation, without
the aid which the institution of money affords.

In other words, most of the rights, services, and commodities, the exchange of which is supposed to be now "facilitated" by the use of money, have never been known to exist even where money itself has been unknown. How then can we be satisfied that money is simply a "medium," when without its influence history proves that there would be but very little between which to "mediate"?

There are implanted in the human mind, over and above the appetites common to all members of the animal creation, certain powerful desires, to the operation of which we can directly trace the conditions of existence in which we now find ourselves. Although it is beyond human ability to explain the ultimate objects served by these innate desires, one fact is unquestionable: and that is, that the desires are so powerful that upon their gratification depends in a large measure the health and happiness of civilised society. These human peculiarities may be roughly generalised under the headings of (1) the various vanities, (2) the love of domination over everybody and everything, (3) the inclination towards material and mental progress, and (4) the workings of those forces usually referred to as religion.

Here we have the leading motives that explain the actions of the great majority of the human family. They are motives that exist alike in the savage breast of the uncultivated and the trained mind of the highly civilised. They have been found continually and more or less powerfully at work in every race of man hitherto discovered. A curious fact about them that is worthy of especial attention is, that so far from their strength being diminished by gratification, precisely a contrary effect is produced. The more civilised mankind becomes, the greater the number and power of the desires that call for attention.

Now in spite of the fact that primitive man has within him the same peculiar motives to industry that are in other and more highly-developed forms influencing the actions of the civilised members of the species, until the institution of money has begun to exert its powers he has nevertheless for centuries remained in that semi-barbarous condition of life, such as that in which European travellers have found the aboriginal inhabitants of America or Australia. But no sooner has that great device been discovered whereby not only can the labours of the human race be most effectively divided, but the products of those labours be as effectually distributed, then the road to progress and civilisation has opened, and those innate motives to industry to which we have just referred have received a stimulus, the power of which it is almost impossible to magnify. Men's desires have increased by leaps and bounds, and with the ability to gratify those desires, fresh and more imperious appetites have been developed. By the legal recognition of certain metals as money, man created an object, the possession of which enabled him to command the services of his fellow-men, and so to further minister to the insatiable demands of his ever growing appetites. The existence of so fascinating an object impelled all men to labour at the most arduous kinds of work in order to secure that by which they could so readily feed their innumerable hopes, vanities, and passions ; and in this fact we have an explanation of the progress of the human race from barbarism to civilisation.

The direction, nature, and incidents of the advance cannot be better recalled to mind than by a consideration of the causes that are at this moment bringing about the rapid development of South Africa or Western Australia. It is discovered that certain comparatively uninhabited regions are rich in that metal of which the great nations of the world now manufacture their money. In consequence of this discovery people from all parts of the world hasten to the spot, and carry with them a multitude of desires that are kept in check simply owing to the absence of money. Money, uncoined, having been found in abundance, the gratification of the desires of all who secure this money follows in due course. Some who have never stirred from London, Paris, Berlin, or New York obtain a large share, but with these we are not at the moment concerned. The demands of those in the neighbourhood of the mines for better food, clothing, and protection against climatic influences, quickly necessitates the importation of commodities from those countries that are more advanced in manufacturing industries than the new money-producing people and their associates. This importation in itself involves special labour to effect the purchase, conveyance, and distribution of the desired commodities. Men and women flock to the scene to supply this labour. The new arrivals bring with them new desires and, if their efforts to obtain money also be successful, irresistible demands for all kinds of rights, services, and commodities. The successful settlers marry, families multiply, and the population (and *per se* desires) increases rapidly. Straggling settlements grow into villages ; villages expand into towns ; telegraphs, railways, steamships, and all the modern appliances of civilised life quickly follow ; and what was, before the discovery of uncoined money, a neglected and barren region, now becomes a thriving, populous, and important State.*

All this comes about owing to the fact that money not only saves time and labour, but, what

* For the influence of Australian and Californian gold on social progress see TOOKE's *History of Prices ;* also R. H. PATTERSON's *New Golden Age.*

is equally important, stimulates industry. The
development of those regions where gold and
silver abound has generally been more rapid
than of those in which the principal attraction
has been mineral wealth of some other kind,
climate, or geographical position. At the same
time, wherever the device of money has been
legally recognised, there men's efforts to obtain
that money have invariably led to a condition of
development impossible amongst those to whom
the invention has been unknown.

Although it would be inaccurate to attribute
to money alone the wonderful growth of the
human family, and the gradual construction
of those vast social and political edifices with
which the world is now quite familiar, it is
nevertheless a fact that the great nations of
to-day, with their powerful military and naval
armaments, their wonderful contrivances for
annihilating time and space, their marvellous
organisations both on land and sea, their
myriads of energetic workers skilled in every
industry, and their countless inventions for
economising labour and promoting of happiness,
could never have existed at all without the continual aid and stimulus which that mightiest of
human inventions—money—affords.

And yet the great economists of the century
have considered money simply in its subordinate
capacity of a time and labour-saving contrivance:
and have argued that its effects upon the human

family are of an exactly similar nature to those
of all other time and labour-saving contrivances !

Money differs from every other invention in
that it is the most powerful stimulus to industry
that has ever been conceived : and this characteristic is one that we must throughout our consideration of the subject, keep clearly in mind.
Although any particular desire of any particular
mortal may be capable of complete satisfaction,
it is certain that the total desires of mankind
are both insatiable and illimitable. As money
is the one and only instrument by the aid of
which these desires can be gratified, it follows
that the desire for money is also without limit :
and this fact explains the influence money
exercises upon the human family. All men
are willing to labour to obtain possession
of that which is the first step (towards) the
gratification of their desires, and this willingness
to labour—this universal striving for money—
constitutes the great stimulus to industry, of
which we find no adequate recognition in the
writings of the great founders of the modern
theory of money.

Necessary as it is to examine the effects
of this stimulus on the prosperity of mankind,
the power of those who possess large accumulations of money is a matter that calls for even
more consideration. Mill regarded money
simply as a "machine for doing quickly and
commodiously WHAT WOULD BE DONE, though

less quickly and commodiously, WITHOUT IT."
The inacceptability of this hypothesis is at once
manifest when we reflect that we have only
to hold forth a handful of sovereigns and we
can cause to be done what certainly would
never come to pass at all, without the incentive
which the desire to possess those sovereigns
affords. And what we can do in a small
measure, capitalists can effect on a large scale.
The fact that England has for many years been
the home of some of the wealthiest capitalists in
the world, explains to some extent the enormous
powers we now command as a nation. A good
example of the result of these powers can be
found in the events that followed the opening of
the Suez Canal. Much of the opposition which
the canal project at first experienced in England arose from the belief that London and
Liverpool would lose their Indian trade, which
then came *vid* the Cape, if a new and shorter
route were opened to the markets of Europe
through Egypt. "The Greeks," said M. de
Tocqueville, "the Styrians, the Italians, the
Dalmatians, and the Sicilians are the people
who will use the canal,"* and this opinion was
widely held both in England and on the Continent. But neither the Greeks nor any other
of the peoples mentioned possessed the MONEY
necessary to bring about the construction of
steamers suitable for the passage of the canal;

* *Vide* BAGEHOT'S *Lombard Street.*

nor had they the MONEY wherewith to command
the transactions that had for centuries been conducted in Liverpool and London. And so we
find that to this day, in spite of England's
geographical disadvantages, over three-quarters
of the produce of the East that is brought
to Europe *via* the Suez Canal, is both financed
in England and carried in English ships.

But the power of money is not even limited
to the production of results such as these. We
all know the story of Aladdin and his Wonderful
Lamp. By simply rubbing the lamp Aladdin
was able to obtain anything he desired; a
mysterious Genius, aided by a myriad of slaves,
executed whatever orders he gave,—supplied
him with choice food and beautiful clothing,
built him a palace of unsurpassed magnificence,
and even transported him in a few moments
from the centre of China to the furthermost
part of Africa.

We are accustomed to pay no more attention
to this story than to any other of the fables
that played on our imaginations in bygone
years. And yet the power Aladdin possessed
was no more remarkable than that exercised by
many mortals at the present moment. The
cheque - book of the modern financier is a
veritable Aladdin's Lamp,—an instrument fully
as irresistible, as useful and as gratifying, as the
mystic utensil of the Eastern tale. The magician
of Lombard Street scribbles a few lines and

thousands of intelligent slaves appear in all parts of the world to do his bidding. He wishes to be transported both rapidly and comfortably to the uttermost corners of the earth. It is done. He desires a palace to be built in London and another in South Africa. It is done. Canals are cut, railways constructed, steamers built, telegraph lines laid, rivers deflected, and even mountains removed, all as he commands. In short, there is no scheme which the ingenuity of man can devise, and which the natural resources of the world render feasible, that the financier of to-day cannot bring to pass, provided he possess sufficient money.

Here, then, we have a Power which knows no equal,—a Power which can be directed towards any end, but which in the present age is generally used for constructive purposes. Should Europe ever again be plunged into the horrors of a great war, this Power will undoubtedly materially influence the result. In such an event the force that can cause cities to arise in a few years, could bring about their destruction in as many weeks. That money should be able to produce such vast results is a matter for the deepest consideration. But Mill — one of the "Fathers of Political Economy"—tells us, "There cannot be intrinsically a more insignificant thing in the economy of society than money, except in the character of a *contrivance for sparing time and labour;*"[*]

[*] *Principles of Political Economy*, Book iii., chap. vii.

F

and around this idea he throws the ramparts of his logic so effectively, that to this day the "medium of exchange" theory continues to hold ground in the public mind.

Sufficient has been said, however, to show that although it is quite correct to describe the cocoa beans employed by the early Mexicans to overcome the difficulties of barter, and all other similarly used go-between commodities, as "media of exchange," such language is utterly inadequate to convey an accurate impression of the part played by the money of to-day in the economy of society. It will be necessary, therefore, if we wish to understand the injurious after-effects of the legislation by which our present system of currency was established, to cast aside the antiquated and misleading term "medium," and find another more in accordance with the powers and influence of the mighty engine that moves all mankind.

CHAPTER VI.

The difference between modern and primitive money—Money
the Great Purchasing Power—A practical theory of money.

HOW can money be best described ? We know it to be (1) the Common Measure of Value, (2) the Common Store of Value, and (3) the GREAT STIMULUS TO INDUSTRY. We have still to recognise its most important function.

Bastiat arrives at what he considers to be the true nature of money in this way : " You have a crown piece. What does it mean in your hands ? It is, as it were, the witness and proof that you have at some time done work which instead of profiting by, you have allowed society, in the person of your client, to enjoy. This crown piece witnesses that you have rendered a service to society, and moreover states the value of it. It witnesses besides that you have not received back from society a real equivalent service as was your right. To put it in your power to exercise this right when and how you please, society, by the hands of your client, has given

you an ACKNOWLEDGMENT, a TITLE, an
ORDER OF THE STATE, a crown piece, in
short, which does not differ from other TITLES
OF CREDIT, except that it carries its value in
itself; and if you can read with the eye of the
mind the inscription it bears you can distinctly
see these words, '*Pay to the bearer a service
equivalent to that which he has rendered to
society; value received and stated, proved and
measured, by that which is on me!*'"

Here we have the essential feature that distin-
guishes modern from primitive money. Modern
money is, with certain limitations, a "right or
title to demand something from others."
(McCleod.) The laws by which its use is
regulated, and the customs upon which these
laws are founded, have made it now impossible
to effectively demand what we require except
by the offer of money. In primitive ages no
man could *compel* others to give him what
he required in exchange for the cocoa beans,
shells, or other go-between commodities then
employed to lessen the inconveniences of barter.
Primitive man bartered as he pleased, and if he
found it convenient to accept beans or shells he
did so. But as soon as the manufacture and
regulation of money became a State monopoly,
the freedom of action on both sides, which was
characteristic of a system of barter, ceased to
exist. By the institution of the law of legal
tender each member of the State was *compelled*

to accept money in discharge of debts due to him ; and further, he was practically enabled to *compel* others to supply him with what he required in exchange for money. Money thus became an ORDER OF THE STATE, which every member of the State was obliged by law and custom to acknowledge.

In rude ages it was only possible for the State to enforce its MONETARY ORDERS by manufacturing them of metals such as silver and gold, which were of great value apart from their use as money. By so doing the people willingly accepted and recognised the force of the ORDERS ; for even if the authority of the State were liable to subversion, the money issued by the State would still be of a value that those who possessed a store of it could readily turn to account. With the advance of civilisation, and the increase of confidence in the power, permanence, and honesty of the governing authority, it became possible for the State to put forth MONETARY ORDERS of PAPER, which served as "titles of credit," Measures of Value, Stimuli to Industry, and Stores of Value almost as effectively as ORDERS of gold and silver had formerly done. But inasmuch as the majority of the world's inhabitants are still without confidence in the permanence of modern governments and the innate honesty of the human race, it has not yet become possible to create that ideal currency of certain celebrated

American writers, the elements of which would possess no value apart from their special use as money.

We are now in a position to see that the money of any given community is the legally recognised POWER whereby we can command both the services and products of every member of that community. Further, that if the money is manufactured of gold or silver, its POWER is so far extended as to enable us to command the services and products, not only of those who are legally compelled to recognise the money, but of practically every people in the world whose products or services we may consider worthy of attention. As the operation of demanding and obtaining what we desire in exchange for money, is popularly known as a "purchase," we can accurately describe gold and silver money as THE GREAT PURCHASING POWER.

At this point a question arises which has caused, perhaps, even more discussion than past attempts to define the nature and functions of money: and this is,—What determines the force or strength of the Great Purchasing Power? Why does money command sometimes more, sometimes less, of the products of man's industry?

The question has been answered by Mill thus : "Money is a commodity, and its value is determined like that of other commodities, temporarily by demand and supply, permanently, and on the average, by cost of production." *Per contra* Mr. McLeod argues that value does not spring from the labour of the producer, but from the desire of the consumer; and that consequently the value of money, like that of commodities, is determined solely by demand and, supply—" by the quantity of it in circulation compared to the operations it represents."

The matter is not difficult of solution if we concern ourselves with facts rather than abstract theories. Some commodities can always be produced at man's will in unlimited quantities; others can only be obtained by "fits and starts," and in comparatively small supplies, no matter how powerful the desire for them may be. Obviously the ultimate value of the latter is based upon demand and supply, and that of the former upon cost of production.

Amongst those commodities the demand for which is without limit, whilst the supply is comparatively small and irregular, are gold and silver. The value of these metals in bygone ages was never measured by the labour expended upon their production (indeed, in many instances, the metals were accidentally found in the beds of water-courses, &c.), but by the strength of the desires of those who wished to acquire them—a strength which the beauty and rarity of the desired object largely influenced. It is the same to this day with rare stones, ancient coins, and all curiosities, the supply of which is irregular and limited. Their value is not in any way connected with their cost of production, but with the desires of those who wish to possess them.

Now the strength of human desire is by no means constant, nor is it even capable of exact measurement. The same pearls which this year may be of great value, are some years hence less esteemed and sought for. The same gold, the possession of which gratifies certain men of the West Coast of Africa, doubly gratifies certain other men of Europe. The quantity of commodities for which the precious metals were exchanged before the adoption of the metals as money, must, in face of such facts, have originally been determined by the strength of the demand of those who desired to possess the metals; and as this demand was incapable of exact measurement, the quantity of commodities generally given in exchange for gold and silver must also have been incapable of exact definition. Such transactions as took place between those who found the precious metals and those who desired to possess them, however, must have gradually led to the establishment of a certain rough exchange value, the limits of which were sufficiently widely recognised to enable mankind by degrees to utilise first silver, and afterwards gold, as instruments of commerce.

And within these limits eventually arose those early monetary values to which we trace the level at which prices generally have now arrived.

We have already noticed that <u>when silver and gold were first used as money, the exchange value of the money was determined by the value of the gold</u> and silver as commodities. We have also noticed that with the general adoption of the precious metals as the principal monetary instruments, the position came at length to be reversed : and at the present day the value of gold and silver freshly unearthed is determined mainly by the purchasing power of the gold and silver money already in existence. Inasmuch as the demand for gold and silver money is unlimited, whilst the new supplies of such money, compared with the stocks already in existence, are not only small and irregular, but at the same time largely beyond human control, it follows that the purchasing power of the money now in existence depends principally upon supply and demand, and *not* upon the expenditure of labour and other matters incurred in the production of that supply.

We thus have two arguments that bring us to this same conclusion, that the value of gold and silver money (that is the strength of the Great Purchasing Power) is but very remotely connected with the cost of the production of the precious metals. It is determined mainly by the quantity in circulation compared with the work it is called upon to perform. The level at which prices generally have now arrived is the result of a long adjustment, the nature of, which we have already sketched. Fluctuations in prices generally, are indications of changes in the strength of the Great Purchasing Power; indeed, such fluctuations are the only evidence we have that the value of money is subject to alteration. If the same quantity of sugar can now be bought for one sovereign which formerly cost three sovereigns, it is evident that the relative values of sugar and sovereigns have considerably altered. The alteration may have arisen (1) from the sugar having fallen in value when compared with commodities generally, (2) from the sovereign having increased in value when compared with commodities generally, or (3) from a combination of both causes. It is evident, however, that we cannot even approximately determine the true nature of the alteration unless we examine the changes, if any, in the prices of commodities generally. If we find that the prices of some commodities have risen whilst those of others have fallen, we can only conclude that these changes have been brought about by something affecting the supply, demand, or cost of production of the *commodities*. But if we find that the prices of practically *all* commodities have risen or fallen,

then it is clear that the change must be due to
something affecting the supply of, or demand
for, *money* which has not similarly affected the
supply of, or demand for, *commodities*.

From the above it follows that if the supply
of money from the mints or from the printing-
presses of Government be greater than the
demand for that money, as represented by the
number and value of the purchases made
amongst any given people, the value of the
money will fall, the strength of the Great
Purchasing Power will diminish, and prices
generally will rise. On the contrary, if trade
and population increase so rapidly that the
demand for money be relatively greater than
the supply of money, precisely an opposite
effect will be produced, and prices generally
will fall.

And now we have a practical theory of
money in place of the old erratic "medium
of exchange" hypothesis, a theory which,
founded both on facts that are past, and on
facts of which we all have every-day experience, will enable us not only to construct
a system of money better adapted to the requirements of the world than the systems
now current, but what is of more immediate
importance, to perceive the consequences to
English trade of the currency legislation by
which our present monetary system was
established.

In answer to the question, What is money?
we can now reply—

Money is:

(1) The Great Purchasing Power.

(2) The Great Stimulus to Industry.

(3) The Common Measure of Value.

(4) The Common Store of Value.

And we can add that the strength of the
Great Purchasing Power fluctuates according to
the quantity of that Power in circulation compared to the amount of work to be done by it.

CHAPTER VII.

The legislation of 1816 examined by the light of a practical theory of money—Effects on internal trade of fluctuations in the purchasing power of money—Effects on international commerce—Conclusions theoretical.

IT will be remembered that when Lord Liverpool recommended his king to outlaw silver and use only gold as England's chief monetary instrument, he was of opinion that this course was the best way by which the inconveniences arising from the disappearance now of the silver coins, now of the gold pieces, consequent upon the different legal ratings of gold to silver in the various States of Europe, could be effectively overcome. And inasmuch as an international agreement to establish one uniform rating of gold to silver was then quite outside the sphere of practical politics, there can be no doubt that Lord Liverpool's recommendations, although supported by historical references that were both defective and inaccurate, nevertheless presented the best means out of the monetary difficulties of the time. Of the truth of this conclusion we can have no letter evidence than

the fact that the inconveniences experienced
during the last and previous centuries are now
unknown with our present currency system;
and this system is to all intents and purposes
the outcome of Lord Liverpool's suggestions.

The ultimate effects upon English commerce
of the abandonment of one of the metals which
had for centuries served as the principal money
of the world, were matters that neither Lord
Liverpool nor Sir Robert Peel could possibly
have foreseen. In those days not only was
international trade as we now see it undreamt
of, but even its coming magnitude and vital
importance to England could not have been
realised; a nation who believed that money
was simply a medium that facilitated the
exchange of commodities, would not suspect
that this growing trade could be in any way
prejudiced by what appeared in the light of
an improvement in the "medium." On the
contrary, such an improvement was calculated
to further facilitate trade transactions and so
prepare the way for an increase in commerce.
Moreover, it must be noted that this view was
apparently supported by facts, for not only was
England's progress during the larger portion of
the present century the envy of the whole of
Europe, but this progress, being attributed in
some measure to England's novel currency
system, caused foreign statesmen to look upon
the new system with favour, and consequently

influenced them in their ultimate resolve to follow England's example and also outlaw silver.

Let us now regard England's currency laws from the standpoint of the practical theory of money set forth in the preceding chapter. As money is the Great Purchasing Power and Stimulus to Industry, what are we to think of that legislation which deliberately abolished a portion of the money which had served England for nine centuries, and which continues to serve a half of the world to this day? Does not such legislation of necessity involve the abolition of a portion of the Purchasing Power of the English nation, and also a portion of that stimulus to industry to the aid of which the nation to a certain degree owes its existence?

Undoubtedly. But we must remember that the strength of the Great Purchasing Power fluctuates according to the quantity of the Power in circulation compared with the amount of work to be done by it. If, therefore, one portion (silver) of the Great Purchasing Power be abolished, it is obvious that unless a supply of the other portion (gold) be made sufficiently large to both take the place of that abolished, and at the same time meet the demands consequent upon increase of population and advance of commerce, the strength of the remaining portion (gold) of the Great

Power will increase, and with it the strength
of the Stimulus which the desire to possess that
Power invariably affords. If we take this fact
into consideration it is quite possible to con-
ceive that whilst discarding silver, although a
portion of the Great Purchasing Power of those
nations who formerly used both precious metals
as money, would be destroyed, the strength of
the remaining portion might, from this very
cause, be so augmented as to leave the ultimate
purchasing power of the nations as a whole
unchanged. In this case the abandonment of
silver would simply have the effect of augmenting the power of those classes who already
possessed stocks of money.

Let us now consider money as the Common
Measure and Store of Value. Anything which
causes the purchasing power of money to
fluctuate, of necessity causes its measuring
functions to be similarly affected. But although the increased strength of the purchasing
power of the gold money of a nation might
possibly make up for the loss of purchasing
power which the abolition of silver money
of necessity involves, the effects upon the
measuring function of the great invention can
by no means similarly counterbalance each
other. An increase or diminution in the
strength of the Great Purchasing Power means
a distortion of the Common Measure and Store
of Value, and this distortion involves very

serious injustices, the nature of which we will now explain.

Let us suppose for a moment that the ton, the gallon, or the yard were suddenly reduced by one-third. All those who had contracted to *buy*, would lose one-third of their purchases, whilst all those who had contracted to *sell*, would make a profit considerably in 'excess of what they had anticipated. If alterations in the standards of weight, capacity, or length were of frequent occurrence, the confusion to commerce would soon become insupportable, and Government would be called upon to fix some definite standard upon which all members of the community could rely.

Now fluctuations in the Common Measure of Value involve injustices no less real, but owing to the absence of information on the subject, the people of England endure such fluctuations without a murmur. The enterprising merchant, having measured the cost of establishing a manufactory, and the probable price at which he can sell the products of his industry, borrows a certain amount of capital which, with that he already possesses, he invests in a new undertaking. Let us now imagine the Common Measure of Value to be mysteriously enlarged. This means that the prices of the products of the manufactory fall; instead of a sovereign measuring ten of the products, as had been originally calculated, it now measures fifteen.

To make fifteen articles requires more time and labour than to make ten, and although raw materials are cheaper, wages, interest, rent, and other charges which have been the subjects of contracts, or the outcome of long-established customs, remain for the time unaltered. The cost of production cannot therefore be immediately altered to meet the drop in prices, and profits are consequently reduced. If the fall in prices be very great, it may result in the complete disappearance of that margin of profit which the enterprising merchant had looked forward to as the reward of his labour and forethought. In this case it will become a question how long the merchant's pride and honour will lead him to lose capital by keeping the manufactory open.

This is but a typical example of the result to all manufacturing industries of an enlargement in the Common Measure of Value. An increase in the value of money will for similar reasons cripple farmers, mine owners, and in fact all classes of producers. At the same time it will *per contra* unfairly benefit all those who possess stores of money, and who derive their subsistence from the interest on money lent to others. The non-producing classes of society, in short, will be able to take advantage of the enlargement of the Common Measure of Value, and obtain forty to fifty inches for every yard due to them.

It follows from the above that a diminution in the strength of the Great Purchasing Power— that is, a contraction in the Common Measure of Value, will bring about precisely opposite effects. All those who subsist upon accumulations of money will be unable to obtain as much of the products of industry as they are fairly entitled to: whilst those who have borrowed capital and who are engaged in active production will obtain more than that share of the profits which they originally calculated would be the reward of their industry.

These considerations bring us to the conclusion that any variation in the Common Measure of Value, any fluctuation in the Great Purchasing Power, in that it inflicts an injustice upon a large and important body of the community, should be most carefully guarded against. If the Common Measure of Value becomes smaller, the constructing and producing classes reap an unfair advantage at the expense of the financing and non-producing classes. On the other hand, if the Common Measure of Value becomes larger, capitalists are able to extract more than their due from the other working members of the community. In the latter instance the great money lenders receive an undue stimulus, and agriculture and manufacturers are seriously checked, possibly ruined: whilst in the former, all industries are unfairly encouraged at the expense of capital. Of the two evils there can be no doubt which is the less from the statesman's point of view. The great financiers of Lombard Street are equally essential to the well-being and progress of the British Empire as are the vast manufacturing and producing industries of other parts of the United Kingdom. But it is obviously better, if fluctuations in the measuring function of money are unavoidable, that those who already possess large stores of value and purchasing power should receive somewhat less than their due, rather than that those who are constructing the industries and material wealth of the country should be paralysed in the midst of their efforts.

So far we have only concerned ourselves with considerations of the possible effects of fluctuations in the Common Measure of Value upon the internal commerce of a nation. Let us now go further and trace the possible effects of variations in the strength of the Great Purchasing Power upon the international commerce of the world.

It will be convenient for the purpose of our argument to assume the world to be divided into two portions, one of which employs silver as its principal monetary instrument, and the other both silver and gold. We will endeavour to discover the consequences to international trade that might be expected to follow the demonetisation by the gold and silver nations of either their gold or their silver.

In the first place let us assume that the gold
and silver nations decide to abolish gold from
their currencies. The whole world would then
be using silver as money: and, consequently,
however the value of this money might fluctuate—whether prices generally rose or fell—no
particular portion of the world would thereby
gain an advantage over any other portion, but
the people of all parts of the world would
be similarly affected. The poor would be
unfairly benefited at the expense of the rich;
the wealth of the rich would be unfairly augmented at the expense of the poor; or, if the
amount of fresh silver unearthed were just
sufficient to take the place of the gold discarded by the gold and silver nations, and at
the same time to meet the requirements of the
increasing population and advancing commerce
of the world, no change in the level of prices
generally would occur: and, consequently,
neither rich nor poor would benefit at the expense of the other, owing to reasons connected
with the currency.

Let us now assume that the gold and silver
nations decided to abolish silver from their
currencies. In this case one portion of the
world would be using silver as its chief monetary instrument, and the other portion, gold. In
the gold countries silver would be simply an
article of commerce in the same way as lead, tin,
and other metals; whilst in the silver countries

it would be the Great Purchasing Power and Stimulus to Industry, and the Common Measure and Store of Value.

Inasmuch as the larger part of the value of the precious metals arises from their use as money, and inasmuch as the purchasing power of money fluctuates according to the quantity in circulation compared with the amount of work to be done by it, one of the first results that we should expect to follow the demonetisation of silver, and the consequent additional work to be done by gold, is an immediate and marked divergence in the relative values of the two metals. In silver countries the value of gold and gold money would increase, and in gold countries the value of silver and silver money would diminish.

At first it would be impossible to accurately gauge the nature of the divergence ; indeed, the fact that one commodity—gold—had risen in value in the eyes of the silver nations, or that one article of commerce—silver—had fallen in value in the eyes of the gold nations, might mean that the demand for gold was greater than the supply, or that the supply of silver was greater than the demand. The only way in which it would be possible to discover whether the money of the gold nations, or the money of the silver nations had varied in its purchasing and measuring functions, would be to inquire whether the level of prices generally had in any way altered.

If it were found that prices generally amongst
the gold nations had remained unchanged, whilst
prices generally amongst the silver nations had
risen, the divergence in the relative values of
the precious metals would obviously mean that
silver had fallen in value not only amongst
the gold nations, but all over the world. On
the other hand, if it were found that prices
generally amongst the gold nations had fallen,
whilst prices generally amongst the silver
nations had remained stationary, the truth
would be that gold had risen in value, not
only amongst the silver nations, but throughout the whole world.

It will be noted that in the above argument
no consideration is taken of the effect of fresh
supplies of the precious metals upon the purchasing powers and measuring functions of the
moneys of the gold and of the silver nations.
There are two reasons for this. In the first
place the annual supplies of gold and silver are
so very small in comparison with the enormous
stocks already in use, that they cannot produce
a very great alteration in the value of those
vast accumulations. In the second place such
temporary effects, as an unusually large or small
supply of fresh silver or gold might produce,
can do no more than very slightly modify the
conclusions already arrived at. That a divergence in the relative values of the precious
metals must arise from (1) an increase in the

value of gold, (2) a decrease in the value of silver, or (3) a combination of both causes, is so obvious as to need no further argument.

It now only remains to set forth the consequences to international trade of a fluctuation in the purchasing powers of the moneys used respectively by the gold and silver nations. If the values of both moneys similarly and simultaneously advance or recede, no effect will be produced on international trade, but similar injustices will be simultaneously inflicted on either the rich or poor of each, and every gold and silver nation.

If, however, the value of one of the moneys remain stationary, whilst that of the other advance or recede, very remarkable results will follow. Suppose for example the purchasing power of the money of the gold nations increases, whilst that of the silver nations remains unchanged. One effect of this increase in the value of gold money will be, as we have already seen, to hamper the advance of every branch of the constructing and producing industries undertaken to supply the internal needs of the gold-using peoples. We shall now see that it will have an exactly similar effect on those constructing and producing industries, the object of which is to supply raw materials or manufactured commodities for the consumption of the silver-using peoples.

As the purchasing power of the money of the

gold nations advances, these nations will be able to buy with the same amount of money more of the commodities of the silver nations than they could before the advance in the value of gold commenced, and at the same time the silver nations will be able to buy, with the same amount of their money, less of the commodities of the gold nations than formerly.

Two results must follow. Owing to the people of the silver nations being able to sell at lower gold prices to the people of the gold nations than they could before the rise in the value of gold, the producers and manufacturers of the gold nations will be compelled to reduce their prices in order to meet those of their silver competitors. Now, a general fall in prices, as we well know, reduces the profits, checks the progress, and tends towards the ruin of both agriculturist and manufacturer. Therefore an increase in the strength of the Great Purchasing Power of the gold nations reduces the profits, checks the progress, and tends towards the ruin of both the internal and foreign agricultural and manufacturing industries of those nations.

The second result is this. As the silver nations are not at the moment able to buy with the same amount of their silver money so much from the gold nations as they could before the increase in the purchasing power of gold money, this disability necessarily causes the silver nations to turn their attention to the cultivation and production within their own territories of such commodities as they were accustomed to buy from the gold nations. Now, the more such commodities they manufacture within their own territories the less they require from gold nations, and the less they require from gold nations the more the manufacturers and producers of the gold nations will suffer from loss of trade. Therefore an increase in the strength of the Great Purchasing Power of the gold nations not only reduces the profits, checks the progress, and tends towards the ruin of both the internal and foreign agricultural and manufacturing industries of those nations, but it at the same time acts as a direct encouragement to the inception and growth of agricultural and manufacturing industries amongst those silver nations, the purchasing power of whose money has remained stationary.

Such are the consequences upon the commerce of the world that must inevitably follow the demonetisation of silver by those nations whom we assumed to be using both silver and gold as money, unless the fresh output of gold from the mines of the world, after the abandonment of silver, be sufficient not only to take the place of the discarded silver, but also to meet the requirements of the increasing population and advancing commerce of the gold-using nations; unless, in short, the level of prices generally, both amongst the silver and gold nations, be undisturbed by the demonetisation of the white metal.

These arguments lead to the following most important conclusions:—

(1) That a diminution in the purchasing power of money unfairly benefits the industrial classes at the expense of the money-lending classes.

(2) That an increase in the purchasing power of money not only impedes the progress of both internal and foreign trade to the unfair profit of the money-lending classes, but that it at the same time stimulates the industries of those nations, the purchasing powers of whose moneys are not similarly advancing.

(3) That of the two evils an *increase* in the purchasing power of money is the more injurious to the well-being, progress, and permanence of a nation.

CHAPTER VIII.

An application of theory to fact—The recent divergence in the values of gold and silver—Cause of this divergence—Nature of the divergence — Index Numbers — Theoretical consequences of fluctuations in the value of money.

A THEORETICAL consideration of the effects upon the commerce of the world of fluctuations in the measuring and purchasing functions of money having prepared the way for a more practical examination of the subject, it will now be possible to accurately read the lessons conveyed by a reference to certain matters of history, in which monetary legislation has had a far greater influence than is generally understood.

At the close of the last century the principal nations of Europe and America were using both gold and silver as money, whilst the peoples of the East and certain portions of the New World carried on their trade mainly by the aid of silver. In 1816 one nation—the United Kingdom—decided to abandon silver and use only gold as the chief monetary instrument. Portugal followed in 1854. Between 1873 and 1878 Germany, Holland, Belgium, Sweden, Norway, Denmark, and the United States of America also decided to discard silver ; and at the same time France, Italy, Switzerland, and Greece closed their mints to the unlimited coinage of the less favoured metal. Since this memorable period Egypt, Austria-Hungary, Chili, and British Honduras have declared in favour of gold, and India has ceased to coin silver.

In general terms it may be said that until twenty years ago Europe and the most advanced portion of America used both gold and silver freely as money, whilst those other portions of the world, the trade of which was of sufficient magnitude to be an object of attention by the great nations of the West, employed silver as their principal aid to commerce. Twenty years ago the Western nations permanently refused to recognise silver other than as a subsidiary form of money, and for twenty years the world has consequently been divided into two parts, one of which has advanced with the instrumentality of silver money, the other under the influence of gold money.

The next matter of history to which it is necessary to give some attention is, that in recent years a most remarkable divergence in the relative values of the precious metals has occurred—la divergence so great and so peculiar that no parallel to it can be found in modern times. In the eyes of those who lived in the East, the value of gold has appeared to rise with a rapidity and to an extent before unknown: whilst to those whose careers were confined to the gold-using lands of the West, the value of silver has seemed to fall with an equally amazing rapidity, and in a similarly surprising degree. Numerous Commissions and International Conferences have investigated the causes of this marvellous divergence in values; but although endless reasons have been given to explain the rise in gold (as some contended), or the fall in silver (as others insisted), the results have been unsatisfactory, and the practical outcome on monetary legislation nil.

In order to arrive at a definite conclusion as to the cause and effects of the variation in the relative values of the precious metals, it will be necessary to make a brief examination of the matter by the aid of the propositions laid down in a former chapter. The following figures show the alteration in values which has attracted so wide an attention :—

Year.	Average Price of SILVER per oz. in London. Pence.	Average Price of the SOVEREIGN in Bombay. Rs. As. Pies.			Year.	Average Price of SILVER per oz. in London. Pence.	Average Price of the SOVEREIGN in Bombay. Rs. As. Pies.		
1867	$60\frac{1}{16}$	10	14	7	1882	$51\frac{5}{8}$	12	2	—
1868	$60\frac{1}{2}$	10	8	—	1883	$50\frac{9}{16}$	12	6	11
1869	$60\frac{7}{16}$	10	8	6	1884	$50\frac{5}{8}$	12	6	4
1870	$60\frac{9}{16}$	10	8	11	1885	$48\frac{5}{8}$	12	15	2
1871	$60\frac{1}{2}$	10	13	7	1886	$45\frac{3}{8}$	13	14	3
1872	$60\frac{5}{16}$	10	8	—	1887	$44\frac{5}{8}$	14	2	3
1873	$59\frac{1}{4}$	10	10	9	1888	$42\frac{7}{8}$	14	15	3
1874	$58\frac{5}{16}$	10	14	7	1889	$42\frac{11}{16}$	14	11	7
1875	$56\frac{7}{8}$	10	15	7	1890	$47\frac{11}{16}$	13	3	4
1876	$52\frac{3}{4}$	11	3	7	1891	$45\frac{1}{16}$	14	1	—
1877	$54\frac{13}{16}$	11	2	6	1892	$39\frac{13}{16}$	15	13	9
1878	$52\frac{9}{16}$	11	4	7	1893	$35\frac{5}{8}$	16	2	—
1879	$51\frac{1}{4}$	12	5	1	1894	$28\frac{15}{16}$	17	15	9
1880	$52\frac{1}{4}$	12	1	4	1895	$29\frac{7}{8}$	18	3	2
1881	$51\frac{11}{16}$	12	3	2	1896	$30\frac{3}{4}$	16	14	2

We have already had occasion to note that
the value of gold and silver at the present day
is but very remotely connected with cost of
production; that it depends mainly on the
purchasing powers of gold and silver money;
further, that the strength of the purchasing
power of money fluctuates in accordance with
variations in the supply of, and demand for,
metallic money. It follows, therefore, that the
values of gold and silver are now mainly influenced by the supply of and demand for
metallic money: and that the recent divergence in the relative values of the precious
metals must consequently arise from some
cause, affecting (*a*) the supply of metallic
money, (*b*) the demand for metallic money,
or (*c*) a combination of both causes.

(With regard to the supply of metallic money,
both the gold nations of the West and the silver
nations of the East are dependent upon the
outputs of the various gold and silver mines of
the world. In estimating the influence of these
outputs upon the purchasing powers of gold
and silver, we must not fail to notice the proportion they bear to the stocks of the precious
metals already in use. The following table is
taken from Dr. Soetbeer's great work,* and
shows the estimated value of the world's

* *Materialien zur Erläuterung und Beurteilung der wirt-
schaftlichen Edelmetallverhältnisse und der Währungsfrage.*
Berlin, 1886.

production of gold and silver from the end of the fifteenth century to 1895.

THE WORLD'S PRODUCTION OF GOLD AND SILVER.

YEARS.	GOLD. £		SILVER. £
1493–1850 . . .	662,900,000	...	1,471,650,000
1851–1885 . . .	890,500,000	...	479,850,000
	£1,553,400,000	...	£1,951,500,000
1886–1895 . . .	276,224,680*	...	229,306,600*
Total Stock .	£1,829,624,680	...	£2,180,806,600

Deducting one-fourth† from the above as an allowance for loss and wear, the following figures give the production of gold and silver for quinquennial periods since 1866, together with the proportion that the annual supply has borne to the stocks of the precious metals already in use.

PRODUCTION OF GOLD AND SILVER SINCE 1866.

YEARS.	GOLD. £	Percentage of ANNUAL Production to stock already in use.	SILVER. £	Percentage of ANNUAL Production to stock already in use.
1866–70 .	129,614,000	. 3 ...	57,224,200	. 1
1871–75 .	103,120,800	. 2 ...	79,607,260	. 1
1876–80 .	110,391,120	. 2 ...	81,462,900	. 1
1881–85 .	102,115,380	. 2 ...	95,089,220	. 1
1886-90 .	112,894,720	. 2 ...	106,672,300	. 1
1891–95 .	163,329,960	. 2½ ...	122,634,300	. 1½

* The figures for 1886-1895 are calculated from the tables of the World's Production of the Precious Metals given by the Director of the United States Mint in his Report of 1896.

† The amount of this deduction is suggested by the allowance taken in the Final Report of the Gold and Silver Commission of 1886.

Even if it be assumed for the sake of argument that cost of production determines the exchange values of the precious metals, the above figures show very clearly that a fluctuation in the cost of producing the annual supply of gold and silver could have little or no effect upon the values of the vast stocks already in the market. The above figures also prove conclusively that variations in the cost or amount of an annual supply, which has never exceeded 3 per cent. of the gold and $1\frac{1}{2}$ per cent. of the silver already in use, could never have caused the value of the whole stock of the former metal to have risen 40 per cent., or that of the latter to fall 50 per cent. The hypothesis that the recent divergence in the relative values of the precious metals has arisen owing to some cause affecting the supply of metallic money, must therefore be rejected on the ground that no evidence exists to support it.*

This conclusion lends support to the alternative proposition that the divergence must have its origin in some variation in the demand for metallic money. The demand for money is the sum total of the desires of mankind, and whether this demand be wholly for metallic money, or in part for promises to pay metallic money, it is obvious that the need

* See in this connection Part I. of the *Final Report of the Gold and Silver Commission of* 1886.

for metallic money will vary in exactly the same direction as the demand for money of all kinds and descriptions.

It is a matter of common knowledge that the nations of both East and West have not remained stationary during the present century ; in population, commerce, and civilisation, all have steadily advanced. This general movement in the direction of increased trade, increased mental cultivation, and increased populations, has involved an enormous increase in the sum total of human desires, and therefore, as these desires can only be gratified by the agency of money, an enormous increase in the demand for money. The nations of the East have required vast supplies of silver money, and those of the West even larger supplies of both silver and gold money.

How have these growing demands been satisfied ? The nations of the East have continued to absorb silver in annually increasing quantities; but the nations of the West, who had for centuries been using both gold and silver, passed certain laws between 1873 and 1878 whereby one channel of demand was stopped—silver was demonetised—and their growing necessity for money was then met, not by the opening of any new channel for the supply of Purchasing Power of some other description, but by a continued absorption of the one metal, the possession of which was the only means whereby commerce

could be advanced and the welfare of the West
carried forward.

The alteration in the demand for silver, consequent upon thirteen of the principal nations of
the world closing their mints to the metal, and
so erecting an effective barrier in the way of its
endless consumption, might be expected to produce some effect upon its value. When the
facts are recalled to mind that a very remarkable change in the relative values of gold and
silver has actually taken place—that the com-
mencement of this divergence dates from the
very period at which eleven of the great nations
of the West outlawed silver—that no alteration
in the rate of the supplies of the precious metals
has occurred of sufficient magnitude to explain
the extent of that divergence—that the pre-
sumption has therefore arisen that the change
in values must have its origin in some cause
affecting the demand for metallic money,—
when these matters are all carefully weighed,
it becomes very evident that the currency
legislation of 1873–8 exactly explains the
alteration in the demand for metallic money
for which we are searching. So long as the
mints of the world were open to the unlimited
coinage of silver, the demand for that metal
was without end ; but directly one half of the
world closed its doors to the unlimited reception of the less precious metal, one half of the
demand for silver was considerably restricted,

and one half of the value was consequently
seriously affected.

That the recent unprecedented alteration in
the relative values of the precious metals has
arisen solely from the general abandonment of
silver by the great nations of the West, can
therefore be accepted as beyond question. The
next step to determine is the exact nature of
the alteration. Has silver diminished in value
throughout the world? has gold universally
increased in value? or has a combination of both
changes occurred? When it is remembered
that the precious metals derive the larger part
of their values from their use as Purchasing
Powers, the demonetisation of silver by Europe
and the United States of America, and the
additional demand for gold which that demonetisation necessarily involved, might be expected
to have reduced the value of the former metal
and increased that of the latter. There exists a
means, however, whereby it is possible to discover definitely the true nature of the change,
and this means it will be necessary to briefly
explain.

The values of gold and silver as metals are
determined by the purchasing powers of gold
and silver as moneys. If, therefore, variations
in the strength of the purchasing powers of gold
and silver moneys be measured, the results will
show the nature of all broad variations in the
values of the precious metals. As fluctuations

in the purchasing powers of money are only perceptible in changes in the level of prices, it is to such changes that attention must be turned, in order to determine the true nature of the recent divergence in the relative values of gold and silver.

Movements in the level of prices generally are best registered by what is commonly known as an "Index Number." The prices of a great many commodities are noted at some given period, and fluctuations in the price of each commodity after that period are calculated at so much rise or fall per cent. By combining the results of the variations in the rise and fall of the several commodities selected for examination, it is possible to discover the direction in which prices generally are moving.

Bishop Fleetwood and Mr. Dupré de St. Maur were the first to produce reliable works in which, by showing the prices of various commodities in ancient times, an attempt was made to ascertain the changes in the value of money that had occurred up to the end of the seventeenth century. The subject has since engaged the attention of Adam Smith,* Lowe,† Scrope,‡ Tooke,§ Sir George Evelyn,|| Porter,¶

* *The Wealth of Nations*, Book i., chap. xi.
† *Present State of England in regard to Trade, Agriculture, and Finance*.
‡ *Principles of Political Economy.*   § *History of Prices.*
|| *Some Endeavours to ascertain a Standard of Weight and Measure.*
¶ *Progress of the Nation*, Section iii., chap. xii.

Jevons, * Price, † and many others. The reports of a Committee of the British Association for the years 1887–90, on "The Best Methods of Ascertaining and Measuring Variations in the Value of the Monetary Standard," together with Professor Edgeworth's memoranda attached thereto, give every information on the theory and practical preparation of Index Numbers.‡

Although variations in the prices of individual commodities may arise from causes connected with the supply, demand, or cost of production of those commodities, it is evident that an advance or a decline in the level of prices generally, can only occur owing to the operation of some general cause which, whilst affecting money, does not in the same degree affect commodities generally, or which, whilst affecting commodities generally, does not for some special reason similarly affect money. If prices on the whole advance, the movement obviously signifies that the purchasing power of money has diminshed ; if, on the other hand, prices generally recede, the change is synonymous with an increase in the strength of the Great Purchasing Power.

The following table of Index Numbers shows

---

* *Investigations in Currency and Finance.*

† *Money and its Relations to Prices.*

‡ See also Professor Edgeworth's article in the *Economic Journal* for March, 1894.

the direction in which the value of silver taels
has tended to fluctuate in China since 1873 :—

INDEX NUMBERS OF TWENTY LEADING CHINESE
COMMODITIES AT SHANGHAI.*

Year.	Index No. of the Prices of Chinese Commodities.		Index No. of the Silver Price of Gold.
1873	. .	2000	...	2000
1875	. .	1787	...	2078
1880	. .	1925	...	2275
1885	. .	1854	...	2425
1890	. .	1808	...	2539
1891	. .	1748	...	2621
1892	. .	1761	...	2950

The movement of the Index Number from
2000 in 1873 to 1761 in 1892 indicates that
on the whole prices were somewhat lower in
1892 than in 1873; or, in other words, that the
purchasing power of silver, so far as commodities at Shanghai were concerned, was
slightly greater in 1892 than it was twenty
years previously.†

The India Office Index Numbers of eleven
of the leading imports and of twenty of the
principal exports of Calcutta given below, show
the direction in which prices in India have
tended to move since 1873 :—

INDEX NUMBERS OF RUPEE PRICES AT CALCUTTA.

Year.	Index No.		Year.	Index No.
1873	. .	100	1876	. . 95
1874	. .	105	1877	. . 99
1875	. .	98	1878	. . 94

* Compiled by Mr. Wetmore, of Shanghai.
† Prices generally have advanced in 1895. *Vide* Foreign
Office Report, No. 1803, on the Foreign Trade of China.

INDEX NUMBERS OF RUPEE PRICES AT CALCUTTA—(*continued*).

Year.	Index No.	Year.	Index No.
1879	93	1888	89
1880	98	1889	97
1881	93	1890	96
1882	89	1891	90
1883	86	1892	97
1884	86	1893	104
1885	81	1894	100
1886	83	1895	100
1887	83	1896	99

It will be observed that for eighteen years the purchasing power of silver in Calcutta, as at Shanghai, was somewhat greater than it was in 1874. Since 1894 its purchasing power in India has remained constant.

Mexico is a silver-using nation. Unfortunately it is impossible to obtain reliable statistics of Mexican prices for many years back: but such as are accessible, tend to show that the purchasing power of silver on the whole has not diminished. The following Index Numbers are calculated from the tables of prices given in the United States Special Consular Reports, *Money and Prices*, vol. xiii., part 1, p. 126:—

INDEX NUMBERS OF NINE LEADING MEXICAN PRODUCTS.

Year.	Index No.	Year.	Index No.
1886	900	1893	1282
1889	821	1894	972
1890	893	1895	1057
1891	867	1896(Sept.)	1113
1892	1037		

With regard to imported articles of luxury,

prices are somewhat higher now than in former years, whilst "heavy hardware" and "improved machinery" are cheaper.*

Japan is a silver-using nation, and here, too, prices generally have been steady, with a tendency to rise. So also in the Straits Settlements. In fact, in whatever direction inquiry be made the result is, broadly speaking, the same. The purchasing power of silver amongst silver-using peoples has remained steady on the whole, with a slight tendency—more noticeable in the last few years--to diminish.

Let us now turn to the gold-using nations. With regard to England several reliable Index Numbers have been prepared, in which fluctuations in the prices of between 22 and 100 articles of commerce have been faithfully registered. The averages have been calculated in every possible way. In some instances allowance has been made for the different degrees of importance which different commodities were thought to hold in the nation's commerce: in others allowance has also been made for fluctua-

---

* In summarising the changes in Mexican prices between 1886 and 1896, the United States Statistical Department remarks : "No general change as to food products not exported. Prices subject to great fluctuations. Advance in price of imported articles, except hardware and machinery. Also in prices of coffee, meat, and sugar," p. 212. (Special Consular Reports, vol. xiii., part i.)

† *Vide* Foreign Office Reports, 1779, 1786, and 1811. Since 1893 a distinct advance in the general level of prices has become apparent, and a marked advance in the rates of wages also.

tions in these degrees which might arise from variations in the consumptions of different years. The Index Numbers of the *Economist* newspaper, Mr. Sauerbeck, Mr. Inglis Palgrave, Mr. (now Sir) Robert Giffen, and Dr. Soetbeer are the best known, and were, moreover, accepted by the Royal Commission of 1886. As the broad results brought to light by all the Index Numbers are identical, it will suffice here to reproduce only one series—those of Mr. Sauerbeck.

Year.		Index No.	Year.		Index No.
1851	. .	75	1874	. .	102
1852	. .	78	1875	. .	96
1853	. .	95	1876	. .	95
1854	. .	102	1877	. .	94
1855	. .	101	1878	. .	87
1856	. .	101	1879	. .	83
1857	. .	105	1880	. .	88
1858	. .	91	1881	. .	85
1859	. .	94	1882	. .	84
1860	. .	99	1883	. .	82
1861	. .	98	1884	. .	76
1862	. .	101	1885	. .	72
1863	. .	103	1886	. .	69
1864	. .	105	1887	. .	68
1865	. .	101	1888	. .	70
1866	. .	102	1889	. .	72
1867	. .	100	1890	. .	72
1868	. .	99	1891	. .	72
1869	. .	98	1892	. .	68
1870	. .	96	1893	. .	68
1871	. .	100	1894	. .	63
1872	. .	109	1895	. .	62
1873	. .	111	1896	. .	61

To the above may be added the following

rearrangement of Mr. Sauerbeck's figures,
which, by eliminating the effects of temporary
fluctuations, shows more ˙clearly the general
tendency of the movement in English prices :—

Years.	Index No.	Years.	Index No.
1851-60	. . 94	1870-79	. . 97
1852-61	. . 96	1871-80	. . 96
1853-62	. . 99	1872-81	. . 95
1854-63	. . 100	1873-82	. . 93
1855-64	. . 100	1874-83	. . 90
1856-65	. . 100	1875-84	. . 87
1857-66	. . 100	1876-85	. . 85
1858-67	. . 99	1877-86	. . 82
1859-68	. . 100	1878-87	. . 79
1860-69	. . 101	1879-88	. . 78
1861-70	. . 100	1880-89	. . 77
1862-71	. . 100	1881-90	. . 75
1863-72	. . 101	1882-91	. . 74
1864-73	. . 102	1883-92	. . 72
1865-74	. . 102	1884-93	. . 71
1866-75	. . 101	1885-94	. . 69
1867-76	. . 101	1886-95	. . 68
1868-77	. . 100	1887-96	. . 67
1869-78	. . 99		

The above tables show most clearly that
between 1864 and 1874 prices generally in England were higher than they had been for many
years previously; and that from this period
until the present day, the purchasing power of
England's gold money has steadily increased.

With regard to other gold-using countries, the
following extract from the Special Consular
Reports on Money and Prices in Foreign Countries, vol. xiii., issued by the United States

Bureau of Statistics, will serve to indicate the direction in which the purchasing power of gold money has varied :—

Country.			Change in Prices, 1886–96.
France	.	.	Decline.*
Germany	.	.	Decline.†
Sweden	.	.	General decline.
Belgium	.		General decline.
Austria-Hungary		.	General decline.
Switzerland	.	.	General decline.‡
Italy	.	.	General decline.§
United States	.	.	General decline.

The tables to which reference has now been made clearly establish two facts—that prices generally amongst silver-using peoples are steady, with a slight tendency to rise; and that prices generally amongst gold-using nations, and especially in the United Kingdom, have fallen considerably; in other words, that the purchasing powers of silver moneys have remained constant, with a tendency to diminish; and that the purchasing powers of gold moneys, and especially the money of the United Kingdom, have considerably increased.

Now the values of gold and silver as metals are determined by the purchasing powers of gold and silver as moneys. Therefore the value of silver has remained constant, with a slight

---

* Except in beet sugar.

† "Decline in cereals and pork and in certain raw products for industries; increase in beef between 1886 and 1895, and in many lines of manufactured goods."

‡ "General decline in cereals and bread-stuffs."

§ Especially in food products.

tendency to diminish, whilst the value of gold has considerably increased.

The true nature of the divergence in the relative values of the precious metals is now quite clear. It is not silver that has fallen in value, but gold that has risen. Silver continues to purchase amongst silver-using peoples almost as much as formerly, whilst gold not only purchases more silver than it did twenty years ago, but it commands more commodities generally, as the Index Numbers most plainly testify. To come to the point, since 1873 the purchasing power of England's money has advanced fully 40 per cent., and the Index Numbers, now published by Mr. Sauerbeck and the *Economist* newspaper, show it to be still advancing.

It will be remembered that a theoretical examination of the effects upon the commerce of a nation of fluctuations in the value of money led to the conclusion that *"an increase in the purchasing power of money not only impedes the progress of both internal and foreign trade to the unfair profit of the money-lending classes, but that it at the same time stimulates the industries of those nations, the purchasing powers of whose moneys are not similarly advancing."*

As the purchasing power of the sovereign has steadily increased during the last twenty-three years, it follows that England's gold currency system has not only hindered the development of both her internal and foreign trade, but it has

at the same time directly encouraged the growth
of the industries of all those silver-using and
paper-using peoples, the purchasing powers of
whose moneys have not similarly advanced.

That such is actually the case ample evidence
will now be given.

CHAPTER IX.

Actual results of fluctuations in the value of money on the commerce of the United Kingdom, and on the commerce of certain other nations.

BEFORE turning from probabilities to facts, it is necessary to recall to mind that although the value of the money of the United Kingdom has been steadily increasing for over twenty years, the results upon commerce cannot be expected to show themselves immediately the rise in gold commenced. Industries involving the acquisition of capital, skilled labour, favourable localities, suitable machinery, and costly buildings, are not to be displaced in a moment, even if they prove no longer remunerative. As soon as the fall in the general level of prices begins to be felt, reductions in the cost of production will be made as far as possible, in order to meet the new conditions, and it will not be until the disappointing results of industry begin to act as a check to fresh enterprises, that a diminution in the rate of progress will be noticed. This may take years. In the meantime the industries of those peoples, the purchasing powers of whose moneys have not similarly advanced, will gradually forge ahead; their products will come in competition with those of the United Kingdom, not only in their own countries, but in other markets, and finally in the markets of the United Kingdom itself. The results of this competition can be clearly foreseen. First, those products of British industry, the preparation of which does not require special skill, peculiar machinery, or very large capitals, will be displaced; then, as the benumbing influence of an unjust monetary system continues to operate, those other products, the manufacture of which has only been perfected by years of experience, by the accumulation of most valuable machinery, and by the acquisition of especially favourable localities, will also suffer a similar displacement. Industrial progress will be checked in all directions, and whilst other countries who receive a supply of money more suitable to their commercial needs than Great Britain are advancing by leaps and bounds, the United Kingdom will gradually come to a standstill and then drop behind.

With these preliminary words of explanation as to the directions in which a rise in the value . of money may be expected to exercise its baneful influence, an examination will now be made of the evidence afforded by the Statistical Abstracts and other Returns issued by the Board of Trade. The following table shows the population of the United Kingdom in the years given :—

Year.			Millions.		Annual Increase per cent.
1871	.	.	31·5	...	—
1876	.	.	33·1	...	1·0
1881	.	.	34·9	...	1·1
1886	.	.	36·3	...	·8
1891	.	.	37·8	...	·8
1896	.	.	39·5	...	·9

The annual rate of increase, small as it is, shows signs of retrogression. The fact, however, that the number of the inhabitants of the United Kingdom *is* increasing, ought, unquestionably, to be accompanied by at least a corresponding increase in the trade of the country. And if civilisation is advancing, if the State generally is in a more flourishing condition now than it was in years past, the increase in commerce ought to be even greater in proportion than the increase in population. The following figures indicate the direction in which the commerce of the country is actually going. They represent the total imports and exports of the United Kingdom *per head of population*, and are calculated from Table 25 of the Statistical Abstract for 1896, issued by the Board of Trade :—

1881-85	.		.	£19	12	1
1886-90	·		.	18	12	10
1891-95	.	.	.	18	7	0

Although the quantity of commodities which
£18 7s. would have purchased in 1891-5 might
—owing to the increase in the power of the
sovereign—have been as great as that which
£19 12s. 1d. would have bought ten years
earlier, the figures reveal an ominous change
which the people of the United Kingdom would
do well to study.

The industries of Great Britain and Ireland
may be divided into two classes—the agricultural and the manufacturing. As the former
do not require such costly machinery and buildings, such special skill, and so many years of
attentive labour, to bring to a condition of
perfection as the latter, agriculture will be the
first to suffer from the unjust monetary system
under which all the industries of the United
Kingdom are now struggling. That agriculture
has suffered, the evidence given before several
Commissions, and the frequent Parliamentary
discussions of the subject, have amply testified.*
The following statement from the Board of
Trade Statistical Abstract of 1896 is not without
interest :—

---

* Mr. Everett's interesting speech of July 28th, 1893, on
Agricultural Depression, has been published in pamphlet form,
and may be consulted with profit.

ACREAGE UNDER CROPS IN THE UNITED KINGDOM
FOR THE TEN YEARS 1886-1895 *

Year.	Total. Corn Crops. Acres.		Total. Green Crops. Acres.		Total. Other Crops. Acres.
1886	. 9,878,787	...	4,726,452	...	—
1887	. 9,735,400	...	4,716,679	..	6,026,946
1888	. 9,785,697	...	4,729,191	...	5,979,351
1889	. 9,637,354		4,541,760	...	6,188,502
1890	. 9,574,249	...	4,534,145	...	6,097,210
1891	. 9,443,509	...	4,510,653	...	6,015,037
1892	. 9,328,701	...	4,467,115	...	5,973,456
1893	. 9,171,180		4,462,755	...	5,916,349
1894	. 9,365,877	...	4,486,092	...	5,862,754
1895	. 8,865,338	...	4,399,949	...	6,061,139

The above figures show that instead of any advance correlative with the diminutive increase in population being perceptible, so far as the acreage under cultivation is concerned, the United Kingdom has already lost ground. The retrogression is principally in Wheat, of which over a million acres have gone out of cultivation during the last ten years. The fall in the price of agricultural produce is so generally recognised that it is unnecessary to produce statistical evidence of the fact; but it *is* necessary to refer briefly to the reasons generally put forward to explain the misfortune. Broadly speaking, free trade and reduced cost of production are the scapegoats that have

* Compiled from the Board of Trade Statistical Abstracts for the United Kingdom.

borne the brunt of the farmer's displeasure
and the landlord's vituperation.

The matter is denuded of much of its in-
tricacy if the mind be fixed on the fact that
agricultural depression arises primarily from the
reduced quantity of money which the agriculturist has, in recent years, received for his
produce. It is true that if the fall in the
monetary value of produce be peculiar to
agriculture—if all other branches of industry
be prospering, and the prices of commodities
generally be steady,—the decline *must* have
its sole origin in some alteration in the conditions under which produce is brought to
market and sold. The cost of production *must*
in some way have been reduced, either by the
removal of legislative restriction—such as the
repeal of the Corn Laws—or by the opening
up of new sources of supplies, and by increased
facilities in the cost and methods of transit.
But if the fall in monetary values be not
confined to agriculture, if the decline in prices
be similarly evident in all branches of commerce
(as the Index Numbers show to be the case),
then it follows that neither free trade, nor any
other reason connected with reductions in the
cost of bringing produce to the markets of
the United Kingdom, is sufficient *in itself* to
explain the retrogression in the agricultural
industries of the country. It follows—granted
that new markets for supplies *have* been opened,

new and improved methods of transit *have*
been devised, &c.—that the knowledge and
energy which have reduced the value of agricultural produce by lessening the cost of production, have not, at the same time, reduced
the value of that for which agricultural produce
is exchanged, *i.e.*, money, by proportionately
increasing the supply; and that consequently
the result of this neglect has been a relative
increase in the value of money—an increase
which expresses itself in a fall in the level of
prices generally. This is the key of the whole
difficulty. This is the secret of the diminution
in the exports from the United Kingdom involved in the following figures :—

EXPORTS FROM THE UNITED KINGDOM.

Year.	Domestic Produce.		General Exports.
	£		£
1874 . .	239,558,000	...	297,650,000
1884 . .	233,025,000	...	295,968,000
1894 . .	215,824,000	...	273,786,000

Whilst the industries of the United Kingdom
have been checked by the increase in the value
of money, countries, the purchasing functions of
whose Great Power have not similarly advanced
in strength, have progressed as follows :—

EXPORTS OF DOMESTIC PRODUCE.

Year.	From India.*	From Argentine Republic.†	From Japan.†
	£	£	£
1874	—	... 8,621,000	... 3,912,000
1879	—	... 9,872,000	... 5,706,000
1884	89,186,397	... 13,606,000	... 6,035,000
1889	98,833,879	... 18,029,000	... 10,631,000
1894	110,603,562	... 20,338,000	... 12,276,000
1896	118,605,745	... —	... —

Although it would be manifestly wrong to assume that a country of the area and in the condition of development of the United Kingdom could have, under any monetary conditions, doubled its exports of produce in the last twenty years, it is not too much to contend that the kingdom ought not to have lost ground, and that too in spite of an increase of population.

That the exports of India, Japan, and the Argentine Republic have been specially stimulated by the rise in the value of gold money may be gathered from an examination of the statistics regarding the exports of domestic produce from the United States :—

* Total value of Exports by Sea from the Board of Trade Statistical Abstracts for the several Colonial and other Possessions of the United Kingdom, 1874-1896.

† From the Board of Trade Statistical Abstracts for the Principal and other Foreign Countries, 1874-1896.

EXPORTS OF DOMESTIC PRODUCE FROM THE
UNITED STATES.*

Year.				£
1874	.	.	.	118,632,000
1879	.	.	.	145,488,000
1884	.	.	.	151,034,000
1889	.	.	.	152,142,000
1894	.	.	.	181,084,000

Although the people of the United States are exceptionally enterprising and energetic, and although they have had very great facilities for the rapid development of extensive and fertile lands, they have not been able to increase their exports of domestic produce in the same degree as certain other peoples who have not made gold their principal monetary instrument.

Let us now turn to an examination of that class of industries the successful prosecution of which requires special skill, great experience, valuable machinery and buildings, and in some instances special localities, in which large supplies of pure water are required, or convenient canals or rivers are absolutely necessary. Such industries cannot, for obvious reasons, be quickly displaced, and consequently, although handicapped by an unjust monetary system, their decline must be very gradual. Such are the manufacturing industries.

* From the Board of Trade Statistical Abstracts for the Principal and other Foreign Countries, 1874-96.

In manufactures the United Kingdom has long held the foremost position in the world. That manufactures must suffer in company with agriculture, owing to an increase in the value of money, has already been theoretically demonstrated. That the manufactures of the United Kingdom have already begun to feel the effects of the power that is oppressing them, the following figures clearly show :—

TOTAL EXPORTS OF BRITISH AND IRISH ARTICLES MANU-
FACTURED AND PARTLY MANUFACTURED.*

Year.	£	Year.	£
1883	215,030,020	1890	229,868,743
1884	208,433,776	1891	214,532,324
1885	189,192,139	1892	196,621,502
1886	190,040,569	1893	189,810,094
1887	198,524,291	1894	184,647,441
1888	209,276,736	1895	195,992,861
1889	219,667,622		

Instead of an increase, at least in proportion to the increase in population, the above table shows that in manufactures, as in agriculture, the United Kingdom is losing ground, and that, too, even if allowance be made for the increase in quantities arising from the fall in prices, which figures, giving monetary values only, fail to disclose. The check to industry is not confined to one particular class of manufactures, but is evident in all directions in which other nations, whose moneys have not recently in-

* Compiled from the Board of Trade Monthly Trade and Navigation Accounts.

creased in power, have up to the present acquired the experience necessary to enable them to successfully manufacture on their own account.

EXPORTS IN DETAIL OF BRITISH AND IRISH ARTICLES MANUFACTURED AND PARTLY MANUFACTURED.*
(In millions of £s.)

Year.	Yarns and Textile Fabrics.	Metal Manufactures, except Machinery.	Machinery and Mill Work.	Apparel and Articles of Personal Use.	Chemicals and Chemical and Medicinal Preparations.	All other Articles Manufactured or Partly Manufactured.	Parcel Post.
1883	111·4	40·5	13·4	11·3	7·8	30·5	—
1884	109·9	37·2	13·0	10·8	7·8	29·7	—
1885	101·9	31·7	11·0	10·3	7·0	27·2	—
1886	105·4	31·7	10·1	9·8	6·7	26·4	—
1887	103·1	34·9	11·1	10·2	7·0	27·1	—
1888	108·9	37·2	12·9	11·2	7·4	31·0	·7
1889	110·2	40·9	15·3	11·4	7·9	33·0	·9
1890	112·4	45·2	16·4	11·3	8·9	34·6	1·0
1891	106·0	39·2	15·8	11·3	8·9	32·2	1·1
1892	100·0	33·0	13·9	10·4	8·6	29·6	1·0
1893	96·6	30·8	13·9	9·5	8·7	29·2	1·0
1894	96·0	28·0	14·2	8·7	8·5	28·1	1·1
1895	101·4	28·9	15·2	9·3	8·3	31·5	1·3

Even in a special manufacturing industry, in which, for obvious reasons, rival countries are unable to at once compete, the United Kingdom appears to have reached that point whence retrogression begins :—

* Extracted from the Board of Trade Monthly Trade and Navigation Accounts.

TOTAL TONNAGE OF SAILING AND STEAM VESSELS BUILT
IN THE UNITED KINGDOM, 1883–95.*

Year.	Total Tonnage, excluding Vessels built for Foreigners and of Vessels built for Her Majesty's Navy.	Total Tonnage of Vessels built for Foreigners, for War and Mercantile Purposes.	Grand Total Tonnage.
1883	768,576	123,640	892,216
1884	497,442	90,832	588,274
1885	405,386	35,626	441,012
1886	293,000	38,528	321,528
1887	306,719	70,479	377,198
1888	483,141	90,806	573,947
1889	671,505	183,224	854,729
1890	652,013	160,625	812,638
1891	670,599	138,894	809,493
1892	692,791	108,757	801,548
1893	495,288	89,386	584,674
1894	574,616	94,876	669,492
1895	519,622	128,012	647,634

Although the demand for manufactured commodities in all parts of the world is ever expanding, and although the United Kingdom has the experience, the machinery, and the capital that should enable her best to meet and satisfy this demand, her exports of articles manufactured and partly manufactured show no signs of the advance that is perceptible in other quarters where different monetary systems prevail. For example, in Japan exports of manufactured goods and of Coal are increasing by leaps and bounds :—

* From the Board of Trade Statistical Abstracts for the United Kingdom, 1883-1896.

JAPANESE EXPORTS OF COAL, AND OF CERTAIN MANUFACTURED ARTICLES.*

(In millions of Yen.)

Year.	Coal and Fuel.	Silk Goods.	Cotton Goods.	Matches, &c.	Wood and Bamboo.	Pottery and Porcelain.	Umbrellas, Toilet Articles, and Fans.	Lacquer Ware.	Paper.
1885	2·0	·3	·2	·1	·3	·7	·2	·5	·2
1886	2·2	·8	·2	·4	·5	1·0	·3	·6	·2
1887	2·4	1·5	·2	1·0	·7	1·4	·4	·6	·2
1888	3·2	1·7	·2	·8	·8	1·4	·5	·6	·3
1889	4·4	3·0	·2	1·2	·7	1·5	·4	·6	·3
1890	4·9	3·9	·2	1·6	·8	1·4	·5	·6	·4
1891	4·8	4·8	·4	1·9	1·3	1·4	·6	·6	·4
1892	4·7	8·3	·8	2·3	1·8	1·7	·8	·5	·5
1893	4·9	8·4	1·8	3·6	2·7	1·9	1·1	·7	·5
1894	6·7	13·0	4·2	3·9	3·3	1·8	1·2	·8	·7

The same in India :—

INDIAN EXPORTS OF CERTAIN MANUFACTURED ARTICLES.†

(In millions of £s.)

Year.	Cotton Twist and Yarn.	Cotton Manufactured Goods.	Jute Manufactures.	Oils.	Woollen Manufactures.	Provisions.
1887	3·4	2·4	1·2	·5	·13	·6
1888	4·1	2·8	1·7	·5	·17	·7
1889	5·3	2·9	2·6	·5	·20	·7
1890	5·8	2·7	2·8	·6	·18	·8
1891	6·6	2·9	2·5	·6	·17	·8
1892	5·9	3·1	2·5	·6	·17	·9
1893	6·9	3·1	3·2	·6	·18	·9
1894	5·1	2·9	3·4	·5	·22	1·0
1895	5·8	3·6	4·2	·8	·21	1·0
1896	6·8	3·4	4·7	·7	·24	1·0

* From the Board of Trade Statistical Abstracts for the Principal and other Foreign Countries, 1885-1896. The export of Cleaned Silk has advanced from 13 millions of Yen in 1885 to 39 millions in 1894!

† Compiled from the Board of Trade Statistical Abstracts for the Colonial and other Possessions of the United Kingdom, 1887-1896. The amount of Coal unearthed in India in 1895 was 3,167,426 tons as compared with 1,130,242 tons in 1882!

And the same in the United States, whose monetary system, though nominally the same as that of the United Kingdom, is very different in practice :—

UNITED STATES EXPORTS OF CERTAIN MANUFACTURED ARTICLES.*

(In millions of Dollars.)

Year.	Iron and Steel Goods.		Cotton Goods.		Agricultural Implements.		Chemicals. Drugs, Dyes, and Medicines.		Coal.
1885	16·6	...	11·8	...	2·6	...	4·8	...	4·6
1886	15·7	...	14·0	...	2·4	...	5·3	...	4·2
1887	16·0	...	14·9	...	2·1	...	5·3	...	4·5
1888	17·8	...	13·0	...	2·6	...	5·6	...	6·3
1889	21·1	...	10·2	...	3·6	...	5·5	...	6·7
1890	25·6	...	10·0	...	3·9	...	6·2	...	6·9
1891	28·9	...	13·6	...	3·2	...	6·5	...	8·4
1892	28·8	...	13·2	...	3·8	...	6:7	...	8·6
1893	30·1	...	11·8	...	4·7	...	6·8	...	10·0
1894	29·2	...	14·3	...	5·0	...	7·4	...	11·9

Year.	Copper Ingots, Bars, and Old.		Machinery.		Leather.		Wooden Manufactures.		Wire.
1885	5·3	...	3·8	...	9·7	...	4·8	...	·2
1886	2·5	...	3·7	...	8·7	...	4·7	...	·3
1887	1·9	...	4·6	...	10·4	...	4·6	...	·4
1888	3·7	...	5·5	...	9·6	...	5·3	...	·5
1889	2·2	...	7·1	...	10·7	...	7·1	...	·6
1890	2·2	...	9·0	...	12·4	...	6·5	...	·8
1891	4·4	...	9·8	...	13·3	...	6·0.	...	·9
1892	6·9	...	10·2	...	12·1	...	6·0	...	·9
1893	4·2	...	10·4	...	11·9	...	6·1	...	1·2
1894	19·2	...	10·4	...	14·3	...	6·8	...	1·1

* Compiled from the Board of Trade Statistical Abstracts for the Principal and other Foreign Countries, 1885-1896.

If these countries are able to push forward
their exports of manufactured commodities so
rapidly, why are the exports of the United
Kingdom at a standstill? The inevitable consequence of the rapid growth of the manufacturing industries of those countries, the purchasing
power of whose money has not advanced in the
same degree as that of the United Kingdom, is,
that the manufactures of the United Kingdom
must be gradually displaced. The following
figures are from the Board of Trade Memorandum presented to Parliament in January,
1897 :—

PROPORTION OF IMPORTS FROM THE UNITED KINGDOM TO
THE TOTAL IMPORTS OF THE FOLLOWING GROUPS OF
COUNTRIES :—

Countries.	Average of 1884-85. Per cent.	Average of 1890-92. Per cent.	Average of 1893-95. Per cent.
United States Argentine Republic Uruguay and Chili	26	25	24
China	25	21	18
Japan	45	34	33
Egypt	39	37	34
India *	77	72	73

As the fall in prices continues to hamper the
industries of the United Kingdom, the home

* Calculated from the Statistical Abstract for the year 1896.
N.B.—The Indian Mints were closed to the free coinage of
silver in 1893.

manufactures will gradually lose ground in the
markets of the whole world.   Thus :—

PROPORTION OF IMPORTS FROM THE UNITED KINGDOM
   TO THE TOTAL IMPORTS OF THE FOLLOWING GROUPS
   OF COUNTRIES :—

Countries.	Average of 1884–85. Per cent.	Average of 1890–92. Per cent.	Average of 1893–95. Per cent.
Europe (excluding Austria-Hungary *) . .	18	... 17	... 16
British Possessions .	54	... 51	... 52

The above tables show very clearly that
*although commerce is everywhere increasing, the
proportion of the increase secured by the manufacturers of the United Kingdom is steadily
diminishing.*

Sufficient figures have now been given to
prove that whilst the industries of certain countries, the value of whose moneys has not
fluctuated in the same degree as that of the
United Kingdom, are year by year rapidly
advancing, agriculture and manufactures in
Great Britain and Ireland are all but at a standstill.   The arguments advanced in a former
chapter would lead to the expectation that the
check to productive industry which a gold
monetary system now involves would not only
be felt in the United Kingdom, but also in other
nations who employ similar systems of money.
That such is actually the case the following

* The Austro-Hungarian Trade Accounts did not show
countries of origin of imports previous to 1891.

figures from Sir Courtenay Boyle's recent Memorandum on the Comparative Statistics of Population, Industry, and Commerce in the United Kingdom, and some Leading Foreign Countries, tend to prove :—

PROPORTION OF IMPORTS INTO JAPAN FROM THE UNDER-MENTIONED COUNTRIES, TO THE TOTAL IMPORTS OF JAPAN.

From	Average of 1884-85. Per cent.		Average of 1890-92. Per cent.		Average of 1893-95. Per cent.
France	5	...	5	...	4
United States	9	...	9	...	8
Germany	7	...	8	...	7

It may be of use here to give an example of the exact way in which the recent rise in the value of gold affects British commerce. Forty per cent. of the cloth made in Lancashire is purchased by India, and consequently anything which tends to restrict the Indian demand seriously affects the great manufacturing county. Until about twenty years ago a rupee was the equivalent of two shillings, and a piece of cloth which the English manufacturer valued at, say, one sovereign in Bombay, the native of India could buy for about ten rupees. Europe having outlawed silver, the value of gold was thereby so increased that to purchase a sovereign in order to pay for a piece of cloth of that price, the native of India has had to give as much as eighteen rupees. Although an increase in the value of the sovereign presumes a reduction in

the price of cloth, the manufacturers of Lancashire are as reluctant to lower their prices as the
buyers of India are to increase the number
of rupees they pay for goods. In practice the
difficulty adjusts itself as follows :—The buyers
of India are very desirous of cloth, and the
manufacturers of Lancashire, who have invested
their money in, and derive their existence from,
cloth mills, are similarly desirous of Indian
custom. Concessions are made on both sides
that enable business to be carried on for the
time being ; manufacturers lower their prices to
a certain extent, and buyers increase the
number of rupees they offer. Two remarkable
tendencies are at once established. In Lancashire the fall in prices tends to check enterprise
by reducing profits, whilst in India the rise
in prices tends to stimulate industry, and lead
native manufacturers to erect mills in their own
country. And with this result :—

TOTAL EXPORTS OF COTTON MANUFACTURED GOODS.

Years.	From United Kingdom. £	Decrease in Value. Per cent.	From India. £	Increase in Value. Per cent.
1881–85	305,838,744	—	12,361,302	—
1886–90	298,159,617	2·5	15,799,317	27
1891–95	282,929,243	5·0	17,956,421	14

TOTAL EXPORTS OF COTTON YARNS TO THE FAR EAST.

Years.	FROM UNITED KINGDOM TO CHINA, HONGKONG, AND JAPAN.		FROM INDIA TO CHINA, HONGKONG, AND JAPAN.	
		DECREASE (−) or INCREASE (+) in Quantity.		INCREASE in Quantity.
	lbs.	*Per cent.*	*lbs.*	*Per cent.*
1875-81	232,304,895	—	117,851,376	—
1882-87	202,093,200	− 13	427,914,265	263 !!
1888-93	206,019,000	+ 2	862,976,237	102 !

As these consequences are produced not so much by a diminution in the value of silver as by an increase in the value of gold, the result is that the ultimate rise in prices in India is very trifling, whilst the ultimate fall in prices in the United Kingdom is very great. And so the manufacturers of the United Kingdom are severely handicapped, whilst the manufacturers of India are effectively stimulated. This same result is produced in all countries, the value of whose money has not increased in the same degree as that of the English sovereign, and who derive their supplies of manufactured goods from the United Kingdom.

Although advancing knowledge and improved methods of communication, combined with the cheap labour, the cheap land, and the climatic advantages of certain foreign countries, will probably render Great Britain's occupation of the markets of the world a matter of gradually increasing difficulty, is it not unwise to artificially increase the difficulty by the employment of a monetary system which not only

K

hampers home industries, but which at the same
time directly stimulates the industries of several
foreign nations with whom the people of the
United Kingdom are in continual competition ?
If such a course be possible, ought not England's
legislators to rather construct a monetary system
by means of which the natural advantages
certain Eastern and other nations possess might
be neutralised, and the commercial supremacy
of Great Britain maintained ?

CHAPTER X.

Actual results on the progress of the United Kingdom of a
deficiency of Purchasing Power and Stimulus—Actual results
of a more adequate Stimulus on the progress of the United
States.

SUCH references to facts as we have already made, show beyond all question that England's present currency system—based as it is upon a metal the value of which is steadily increasing—is acting as a most serious check to the progress of the whole of our productive industries. Further, in that the advance in the value of England's money serves as a direct stimulus to every nation, the strength of whose Purchasing Power remains constant, it follows that the existing state of affairs tends to promote the growth of manufactures in many of those countries who have hitherto been accustomed to purchase from us ; and such a growth of necessity involves a loss of trade to England.

But this is not all. Money is the Great Purchasing Power and the Great Stimulus to Industry. And this is true of every kind of money that mankind in any numbers will recognise, be it of gold, silver, copper, or paper. In placing legal barriers in the way of the free and unlimited coinage of silver, the people of England have not only deliberately deprived themselves of one of the greatest stimuli to industry, but they have at the same time rejected the very Power which in a great measure aided in the building up of that civilisation amidst which they now live, and which to this day is the great lever that moves a very large portion of both the Old and New World! Although they know the value of the Wonderful Lamp, and although they can see in East and West the marvellous power of Aladdin's Ring, yet, under the blind influence of an erratic economical orthodoxy, they have cheerfully discarded the less esteemed Ring; and like Aladdin, until they have lost the power they now hold, it seems that their eyes will not be opened to the value of the minor charm.

No man would think of cutting off his left hand because that member was not so useful as his right; yet the rejection of silver as money has precisely the same effect upon the industries of Great Britain as the loss of a limb would have on any individual engaged in those industries. That the prejudicial results of so unnecessary a self-crippling are not at once perceived, arises from the continued acceptance of a fanciful and out-of-date theory, which treats of the Great Power simply as a "medium of exchange." Money is *not* a medium of exchange. Money is *not* an instrument for doing quickly and conveniently what would be done, though less quickly and conveniently, without it. On the contrary, money is an instrument that does what nothing but money could do, and what would therefore never, under any circumstances whatever, be done at all without money. In short, money is a great constructive Power, and to close the mints to the free and unlimited coinage of silver is to deliberately cast aside a portion of that Power.

Unfortunately this fact has escaped the attention of both rulers and ruled, with the result that the people of England, notwithstanding their great progress, are now being outdistanced by those whose energies and industries have not been similarly handicapped.

Reference has already been made to the extraordinary progress of the far East, so attention will now be directed towards a nation of the same inherent energy and propensity for commerce as the British, but whose industrial capacities have not only been spurred to the utmost by a plentiful supply of both silver and gold money, but who have also had recourse to the purchasing power and stimulating influence of a paper currency.

The United States of America decided in 1873 to adopt a gold monetary system on the

same plan as that which was considered to have
been so successful in England. Fortunately for
the welfare of the United States the silver-
producing interests were sufficiently powerful
to bring about certain legislative enactments,
whereby the less favoured metal might be
largely utilised for purchasing and other purposes; and this recognition of the power of
silver as money afforded a motive to enterprise
(especially in the development of the Western
States) that explains in a large measure the
rapid growth of the whole nation.

Up to 1873 the United States freely converted
both silver and gold into money, and so derived
the maximum advantage of that stimulus to
industry which the possession of rich silver
or gold mines has ever afforded.   Although the
more precious metal was legally recognised
as the principal monetary instrument in' 1873,
silver was not discarded in the United States to
the extent that England's legislators had
thought desirable in England, and consequently
the people of the United States possessed
inducements to wealth creation ignored by the
people of the United Kingdom.   The following
table gives some idea of the extent to which
the United States—nominally a gold nation,—
have utilised silver :—

TOTAL COINAGE OF SILVER.

Years.	United Kingdom.* £		United States † £
1876-80	2,567,862	...	27,279,333
1881-85	3,830,140	...	28,531,459
1886-90	6,013,788	...	35,000,597
1891-95	4,998,475	...	12,772,217
Total	£17,410,265	...	£103,583,606

The above figures simply mean that in the twenty years ending 1895, not only have the Americans' inclinations for labour been far more effectively stimulated, but the people have actually been able, so far as silver alone is concerned, to employ nearly six times as much Purchasing and Constructive Power as the inhabitants of the United Kingdom.

The same advantages have been theirs with regard to gold. Not only has the output from the mines of the United States been exceptionally large, but the greater portion of this output has been converted into money at the various United States mints.

TOTAL COINAGE OF GOLD.

Years.	United Kingdom.‡ £		United States.§ £
1876-80	12,128,287	...	48,350,746
1881-85	6,701,200	...	48,749,066
1886-90	19,122,600	...	25,235,968
1891-95	39,386,436	...	52,033,752
Total	£77,338,523	...	£174,369,532

* Compiled from the Board of Trade Statistical Abstracts for 1876-1896.

† Compiled from the Report of the Director of the United States Mint, 1896.

‡ Compiled from the Board of Trade Statistical Abstracts for 1876-1896.

§ Compiled from the Report of the Director of the United States Mint, 1896.

Here, also, the people of the United States have derived the advantages of a more effective Stimulus, and a larger supply of Purchasing and Constructive Power, than the people of the United Kingdom.

The British mind, when out of Britain, is readily able to grasp and appreciate the advantages of a more practical regulation of the currency than exists in England; and the citizens of the United States, who were not slow to perceive the, powers of silver money and of paper certificates representing silver and gold money, very quickly grasped the fact that the same stimulus and power which was derived from such paper money might also be derived to a certain extent from pieces of paper bearing a Government stamp, and representing neither gold nor silver, but simply DEBTS. Such paper money, it is true, carried no value in itself as paper, but the Government stamp upon it showed it to be a STATE OBLIGATION—a GOVERNMENT ORDER—which no member of the State could refuse to recognise, and consequently, *within the limits of the United States*, it could be made to serve as money exactly as those other paper Government Orders, against which reserves of the precious metals were held, had always served. And so this wise people, who had been compelled to issue nearly £100,000,000 in paper promises during their Civil War, decided not to abolish a paper money that had been utilised so effectively, but rather to allow it to continue to circulate—confidence being maintained by the holding of a certain reserve of gold against the paper.*

Under the influence and by the aid of this plentiful supply of gold, silver, and paper Purchasing Power, the United States have advanced in a way that those who are inclined to congratulate themselves on the progress of Great Britain will find unpleasant to contemplate. The following figures are taken from the Board of Trade Memorandum on the Comparative Statistics of Population, Industry, and Commerce in the United Kingdom and some Leading Foreign Countries, presented to the English Parliament in January, 1897. A reference will first be made to one or two of those principal industries in which Great Britain, on account of her natural resources, her vast capital, the energy of her people, and the acquired experience and appliances of so many generations, might reasonably be expected to bear the palm.

QUANTITY OF COAL PRODUCED.
(In millions of tons.)

	Annual Average, 1870-74.	1890-94.	Increase. Amount.	Per cent.
United Kingdom .	. 120 .	180 .	60 .	50·0
United States .	. 4·† .	153 .	111 .	264·3

* The inhabitants of the States have been familiar with the use of paper money for over 200 years.

† Average of three years—1870, 1873, 1874.

Not only have the United States advanced at a far more rapid pace than the United Kingdom, as shown by the increase per cent., but the absolute increase — 111,000,000 tons — is far greater than the absolute increase in the case of the United Kingdom—60,000,000 tons.

AVERAGE ANNUAL PRODUCTION OF COAL IN THE UNITED KINGDOM AND THE UNITED STATES IN TONS *PER HEAD OF POPULATION*, AT DIFFERENT PERIODS, COMPARED :—

Average of	United Kingdom.		United States.
1870–74	3 79	...	1·09
1875–79	3·97		1·17
1880–84	4·45	...	1·79
1885–89	4·51	...	2·04
1890–94	4·73		2·45

This table confirms the conclusion the increased output in the quantity of coal given above tends to show, viz., that the *United States have advanced more than four times as rapidly as the United Kingdom.*

The next table tells a similar tale, except that where the United States have advanced England has actually receded.

QUANTITY OF PIG IRON PRODUCED.

	Annual Average, 1870–74. Tons.	1890–94. Tons.	Increase. Amount.	Per cent.
United Kingdom	6,400,000	7,300,000	900,000	14·1
United States	2,200,000	8,100,000	5,900,000	268·2

AVERAGE ANNUAL PRODUCTION OF PIG IRON IN THE
   UNITED KINGDOM AND THE UNITED STATES IN TONS
   PER HEAD OF POPULATION, AT DIFFERENT PERIODS,
   COMPARED :—

Years.	United Kingdom.		United States.
1870-74	·20	...	·06
1875-79	·19	...	·05
1880-84	·23	...	·08
1885-89	·21	...	·11
1890-94	·19	...	·13

In the export of domestic produce it is hardly
necessary to bring forward figures to bear
witness to Great Britain's decadence. The
following tables, however, tell the story only too
clearly :—

FIVE YEARS' AVERAGES OF THE EXPORTS OF
   DOMESTIC PRODUCE.
(In millions sterling.)

	Average, 1880-84.	Average, 1891-95.	Increase (+) or Decrease (−).	
			Amount.	Per cent.
	£	£	£	
United Kingdom	234	227	−7	−3·0
United States	166	183	+17	+10 0

ANNUAL EXPORTS OF DOMESTIC PRODUCE, COMPARED FOR
   QUINQUENNIAL PERIODS, *PER HEAD OF POPULA-
   TION*:—

Years.	United Kingdom.				United States.		
	£	s.	d.		£	s.	d.
1870-74	7	7	3	...	2	19	11
1875-79	6	0	0	...	2	16	3
1880-84	6	13	2	...	3	5	11
1885-89	6	3	8	...	2	11	10
1890-94	6	2	11	...	2	19	0

With regard to imports, the following figures show clearly the direction in which the United Kingdom is drifting. Whereas the United States are gradually becoming less dependent upon foreign countries for their various supplies, the United Kingdom is gradually finding it necessary to purchase more and more from abroad.

ANNUAL NET IMPORTS (IMPORTS DEDUCTING RE-EXPORTS) *PER HEAD OF POPULATION*, COMPARED FOR QUIN-QUENNIAL PERIODS :—

Years.	United Kingdom.				United States.		
	£	s.	d.		£	s.	d
1870-74	9	2	4	...	2	18	7
1875-79	9	10	4	...	2	2	5
1880-84	9	15	4	...	2	15	7
1885-89	8	14	2	...	2	8	11
1890-94	9	7	3	...	2	11	11

The United Kingdom has during the whole of the present century ranked foremost in the world for manufactures : and the technical experience, perfected machinery, knowledge of the world's markets, which this position has involved, would appear to afford the best of reasons for concluding that England's manufacturing supremacy would be indefinitely maintained. The following figures show that the United States are progressing far more rapidly than the United Kingdom :—

EXPORTS OF MANUFACTURED ARTICLES.

Year.	United Kingdom. £		United States. £
1883	. .	215,030,020	...	28,000,000
1884	. .	208,433,776	...	28,000,000
1885	. .	189,192,139	...	31,000,000
1886	. .	190,040,569	...	28,000,000
1887	. .	198,524,291	...	28,000,000
1888	. .	209,276,736	...	27,000,000
1889	. .	219,667,622	...	29,000,000
1890	. .	229,868,743	...	31,000,000
1891	. .	214,532,324	...	35,000,000
1892	. .	196,621,502	...	33,000,000
1893	.	189,810,094	...	33,000,000
1894	. .	184,647,441	...	38,000,000
1895	. .	195 992 851	...	38,000,000

That is to say, whilst the United Kingdom has slipped *backwards* 9 per cent. the United States have gone *forward* 35 per cent.

In connection with all the figures reproduced above it must be remembered that fluctuations in the value of money—that is, changes in the level of prices generally—have not been taken into consideration. At the same time, if allowance be made for variations in the bulk of commodities not revealed in statistics of monetary values, the broad conclusion which a comparison of the industrial rates of progress of the United States and the United Kingdom enables us to form, is in no wise altered. With regard to both internal and external trade, the United States have advanced far more rapidly than the United Kingdom.

We need only make one more comparison, and that is in connection with the growth of population. Here are the figures for the last twenty-five years :—

Year.	No. of Population in United Kingdom.		Year.	No of Population in United States.
1871	.	31,500,000	...	1870	.	38,558,000
1876	.	33,200,000	...	1875	.	44,357,000
1881	.	34,900,000	...	1880	.	50,156,000
1886	.	36,300,000	...	1885	.	56,389,000
1891	.	37,700,000	...	1890	.	62,622,000
1896	.	39,500,000	...	1895	.	69,622,000

In the United Kingdom there has been an advance of about eight millions, in the United States thirty-one millions. This increase in population is a matter to which it is necessary to give some attention. When allowance is made for the four and a half millions who have emigrated from the United Kingdom,* and the eight millions who have immigrated to the United States † since 1871, the fact still remains that the people of the United States have not only multiplied at twice the rate of those of the United Kingdom, but their annual rate of increase at the present day is similarly superior. The inhabitants of the United States are in a certain measure of the same race as the people of Great Britain and Ireland. How then is the

* *Vide* the Board of Trade Statistical Abstracts for the United Kingdom, 1871-1896

† *Vide* the Board of Trade Statistical Abstracts for the Principal and other Foreign Countries, 1871-1896.

fact to be accounted for that those who have laboured on one side of the Atlantic Ocean have multiplied and progressed at more than twice the rate of those who have laboured on the other side? So far as energy of character, suitability of climate, and fertility of soil are concerned, the people of the United States have possessed no advantage over their kindred of the United Kingdom. In one respect, however, there has been a great difference. Whereas the lands of the United Kingdom have for many years all been acquired and more or less developed by individual members of the State, many of the lands of North America have, until comparatively recent times, been the property of no individual member of the community, and they have consequently undergone no methodical development. But is the existence of a vast expanse of undeveloped territory in itself sufficient to explain the rapid growth of a nation of the wealth and power of the United States? Seeing that there have been thousands of miles of undeveloped territory in other quarters of the globe, which, although known to mankind, have *not* been the fields of such marvellous operations as North America, and which have *not* become the homes of peoples of anything like the industry of the inhabitants of the United States, must we not look for some more adequate explanation of the remarkable rapidity at which a handful of colonists have built up a mighty nation ?

An explanation can readily be found. The soils of other undeveloped territories, even when fertile, well watered, or rich in coal or mineral deposits, have *not* yielded over two hundred and seventy millions sterling of silver and over four hundred millions sterling of gold in the last hundred years.* Lacking the vast Stimulus and irresistible Purchasing Power which this enormous supply of metallic wealth afforded, the progress of other undeveloped territories, in spite of man's efforts, has been slow, and the results insignificant when compared with those achieved by the people of the United States.

It will be remembered that California and South Australia were not *discovered* between 1850 and 1860 ; the land had always existed, and had for many years been known to the more civilised members of the human family. But no sooner was it reported that a plentiful supply of Purchasing Power might be readily obtained in the undeveloped territories than people hastened from all corners of the globe to assist in the development. Some searched for gold, others turned their attention to the supplying of the wants of the successful searchers. The result of the acquisition of Purchasing Power was a call for commodities of all kinds

---

* *Vide* the Report of the Director of the United States Mint for 1896 upon the Production of the Precious Metals.

and descriptions. Trade flourished not only in America and Australia, but also in the United Kingdom. As the supply of money for the moment became greater, relatively, than the supply of commodities, &c., prices generally began to rise,* industry was stimulated in all directions, commerce rapidly advanced, and a period of general prosperity commenced.

Very similar results have followed the recent discoveries of unmanufactured money in West Australia, South Africa, and elsewhere. Although the undeveloped regions have been known to exist for many years, mankind have only hastened to develop them under the stimulus of a probable acquisition of Purchasing Power. The prospect of possessing an undeveloped country will always attract a few of the more venturesome spirits of the millions of Europe ; but the conversion of such a country into a prosperous, thickly-populated, agricultural and manufacturing State is only possible by the aid of a plentiful supply of money. The people of the United States have had a plentiful supply of money, and to its influence and power the rapid development of American industries is distinctly traceable.

As the United Kingdom is not rich in either gold or silver mines, its people are dependent for their supply of metallic money mainly upon the results of their agricultural, manufacturing, and

* *Vide* the Index Numbers, p. 106.

L

financial operations. Such money as eventually flows into the country represents the balance due for interest on Purchasing Power lent to other countries, for services of all kinds rendered abroad, and for the sale of raw and manufactured products. In checking the influx of silver by refusing to accept as money a metal which all the nations of the East and of certain parts of the West readily recognise and largely utilise, the people of the United Kingdom have deprived themselves of that which in stimulating influence and purchasing power ranks only second to gold. With so extraordinary a renunciation of Power and Stimulus, can we be surprised that in population, in commerce, and in the rate of progress generally, the people of England seem now unable to keep pace with their own kindred in America, Africa, or Australia?

CHAPTER XI.

Conclusions to be drawn from the foregoing—Monetary reform urgently needed—The true nature of money—The direction in which reform should be made.

THE theories employed and the facts already examined show unmistakably that if the agricultural and manufacturing industries of the United Kingdom are to be saved from gradual asphyxia and ultimate comparative extinction, some great monetary reform is urgently needed. Not only is England's commercial progress seriously crippled by the want of that adequate stimulus to industry which a plentiful supply of the Great Power has effectively afforded in other lands, but during the last twenty-five years her advance, such as it is, has been made in the face of a paralysing fall in prices—the visible evidence of an adverse fluctuation in the purchasing and measuring functions of money. These subtle impediments to wealth creation are the outcome of defects in England's currency system—defects which, owing partly to the influence of the great money-lending classes, and partly to the continued acceptance of the fantastic theory of money inaugurated by Adam Smith, it has been impossible up to the present to remedy.

Until the appearance of Smith's great work the people of England, perceiving that money of gold or silver could purchase all that men desired, believed that gold and silver were the principal forms of wealth. As England possessed neither silver nor gold mines, the precious money could only be obtained by encouraging exports of merchandise and restraining imports. The latter was effected by high duties and absolute prohibition, whilst the former was attained by drawbacks, bounties, advantageous commercial treaties with foreign States, and by the establishment of colonies in distant lands. This was the celebrated Mercantile System.

Although the great economists and statesmen of the United Kingdom have ridiculed and swept aside the Mercantile System, there can be no doubt that in principle it was thoroughly sound. The condition of civilisation at which we have now arrived no longer renders it necessary to adopt the methods by which the legislators of earlier ages hoped to enrich their country, but the fact remains that money is still the Great Power—money still purchases practically all that men want; and the actions of the peoples of the world show that money is still regarded as the most desirable and useful form of wealth. Nobody questions that it is to the interest of the individual to receive more money than he pays away. Is it not then to the interest of the mass of individuals who form the State, that more money should be due *to* them than *by* them? Should not the nation as a whole earn more than it spends? And if so, ought not the Legislature to take such steps as may be calculated to bring about this result?

Undoubtedly. Yet this is the old Mercantile System. The only difference between the ideas of to-day and those of a century and a half ago is with regard to the *means* by which the acquisition of wealth can best be encouraged. With the additional security which a more advanced civilisation affords, it is no longer necessary either for the individual or for the State to retain and hoard money of gold and silver. The right to money is, for some purposes, as useful as the actual money itself; and promises to pay gold or silver, or acknowledgments that gold or silver are due, will now serve in many circumstances where before the precious metals were absolutely necessary. But the acquisition of money and of rights to money engages as much attention now as ever the desire for silver and gold did in bygone ages. Whilst economists have been arguing that money is not wealth, but simply a "medium" that facilitates the exchanges of wealth, man has everywhere been striving to secure as much of the "medium" as possible. And where his efforts have proved most successful, there the

race have flourished, multiplied, and advanced
in the greatest degree.

In the meantime the regulation of the
"medium" in the United Kingdom has been
left to take care of itself; with the result that
at the present day the purchasing and measuring
functions of money are undergoing a distortion,
the effect of which is to seriously hamper both
internal and foreign trade, to the unjust gain
of the money-lending classes. Not only have
the industries of the United Kingdom been
retarded by an artificially restricted supply of
the "medium," but such "medium" as the
people have employed has so steadily increased
in value, that both agriculture and manufactures
have become less and less productive. "The
sooner an unproductive industry is stopped the
better, be it agriculture, or mining, or anything
else," is the opinion of one of England's great
bankers.[*] This is a matter of some interest,
however, to the thirty-nine millions of Great
Britain and Ireland who are not bankers; and it
may be that when the facts are understood
by them, a monetary system which benefits the
producing classes at the expense of the great
capitalists may seem a more desirable arrangement than one which has an exactly opposite
effect. If it can be shown that it is in the best
interests of the British Empire that Great

* The late Mr. Bertram Currie.   Reply to Question 6767 of
the Royal Commission on Gold and Silver.

Britain's industrial supremacy should no longer
be an object of solicitude—that the productive
classes should be abandoned, whilst the whole
country be gradually converted into one huge
banking concern, then the most powerful arguments will have been found for maintaining the
present monetary system. If, on the other
hand, it be admitted that a nation's prosperity
and power depends in a large measure upon the
variety and magnitude of its industries, and upon
the growth and number of its population, then it
is imperative that such reforms be made in England's currency laws as will most effectively
stimulate the growth of both commerce and
people.

The time is now becoming ripe for monetary
reform. The industrial classes are at length
opening their eyes to the fact that the competition of the East, and also of other countries
the supply of whose money is sufficient to
prevent a continuous fall in the level of prices,
is not a fair and natural competition, but one in
which the British are hopelessly handicapped
owing to the relative artificial scarcity of money,
created to a large extent by the outlawry of
silver. Many of the great financiers, too, are
now beginning to realise that although an
increase in the purchasing and measuring
functions of money is undoubtedly a momentary
advantage to them, their ultimate welfare is
most intimately allied with the welfare of

those to whom they lend Purchasing Power; and consequently that if the undertakings of the industrial classes are in any way impeded, the demand for loans must of necessity be prejudicially affected. The result must be an artificially created and undesirable surplus of loanable capital, a consequent fall in the rates of interest, and an inevitable diminution of money-lenders' profits.* And finally the public generally, who are now taking an interest in currency matters, are at last grasping the fact that money is not a parcel and part of Nature placed at the disposal of mankind by an unseen providence, and governed by laws that cannot be understood, but that it is a human invention, developed, manufactured, and controlled solely by human power, and that, consequently, the alteration or regulation of the contrivance is a matter upon which every man can bring some influence to bear.

The preparation and issue of money has always been claimed as a kingly prerogative. At the present day in the United Kingdom the matter is one over which the Legislature exercises supreme authority. The nature and extent of this authority may be gathered from the Coinage Acts of 1870, 1889, and 1891.† These Acts, whilst tacitly recognising the

---

* Of the six principal joint-stock banks, there is only one which has not reduced its dividends during the last few years.

† *Vide* Appendices A, B, and C.

necessity of providing the people of the United Kingdom with as many gold coins of a certain weight and quality as the gold brought to the Mint by the public may suffice to manufacture, and whilst also recognising the desirability of issuing sufficient silver and copper tokens to enable petty commercial transactions to be readily adjusted, for which the gold coins would be too valuable, entirely ignore all responsibility on the part of the Legislature to in any way regulate the supplies of money, or control the functions of the great invention! "When the principles which under-lie it are thoroughly understood," says Mr. Alexander del Mar,* "money is perhaps the mightiest engine to which man can lend· his guidance. Unheard, unfelt, almost unseen, it has the power to so distribute the burdens, gratifications, and opportunities of life that each individual shall enjoy that share of them to which his merits entitle him, or to dispense them with so partial a hand as to violate every principle of justice, and perpetuate a succession of social slaveries to the end of time." And yet the English Coinage Acts do not enforce any scientific regulation of the Great Power whatever, but simply provide for an irregular supply of sundry pieces of stamped metal of certain weights and quality. So inadequate a recognition of the influence of a great force is

* *A History of Money in Ancient Countries*, &c.

little short of a disgrace to a nation who have
hitherto dominated the world in everything that
pertains to the material side of civilisation.

Money is the Great Purchasing Power and
Stimulus to Industry, the Common Measure or
Standard of Value, and the universally recognised
Store of Value.   If the currency is to be subject
to intelligent regulation, it is obvious that these
four functions must be closely watched and
continually controlled.   It has been argued that
as the supply of money depends upon the output of gold and silver from the mines, the
matter is to a large extent beyond human
control; and the present currency laws of
England certainly imply as much.   If so, it
would follow that justice between man and
man is also a matter beyond human control—
a contention to which members of civilised
communities will hardly be ready to subscribe.
The truth is that as currency regulation has
received no attention at the hands of the
people, it has been more or less neglected by
the Legislature.   That this neglect should no
longer continue must be the desire of all those
who have the interests of the empire at heart.
A clear understanding of the exact part that
money plays in the advancement of the human
family is the first thing needful.   As soon as
this is obtained, the application of the knowledge to the rational control of the Great Power
will soon follow.

Money is the Common Store of Value. In bygone ages it was the one and only means whereby the surplus fruits of industry could be safely and conveniently accumulated. Then, the money of gold or silver was hidden, or buried in the ground. Now, under the protection of a more advanced, just, and powerful Government, there are many other means by which the surplus products of toil can be permanently preserved; and money is therefore generally used to facilitate the accumulation of wealth by affording a temporary store of value, rather than to serve as a long standing reserve of Purchasing Power as formerly. Further, it is no longer necessary amongst civilised nations that this money should be of a material that will withstand the actions of the elements. So long as confidence is felt in the power and permanence of the Government, paper acknowledgments of monetary debt can be utilised as Stores of Value, just as the precious metals have been so utilised in more barbarous times. The State can recognise and enforce the liquidation of all such paper acknowledgments of debts expressed in monetary symbols, and there is no reason therefore why the law should restrict the free and unlimited coinage of money to *gold only* so far as the store-of-value function of money is concerned. Silver, copper, or paper bearing a Government stamp, would serve equally as well.

Money is the Common Measure of Value. A measure of value ought to be constructed on the principle that underlies the preparation of all other measures. The object of a public Standard is to provide for the use of the people a certain definite, unchangeable unit of length, capacity, weight, &c. Of what that unit consists, or how that unit is expressed, is immaterial, so long as it is immutable and permanent. The essence of every standard of length, capacity, &c., is its fixity; any fluctuation in the standard would at once destroy its utility and lead to fraud and injustice. So obvious is this, and so necessary is it that no alterations should be permitted to occur, that the Weights and Measures Act prohibits the use of any denomination of weight or measure other than one of the imperial weights or measures, or some multiple or part thereof.*

Although money has always been recognised as a public Measure of Value, and although every precaution has been taken to prevent fluctuations in the public measure of length, weight, volume, area, &c., no attempt has been made by England's legislators to control the Standard of Value. Index Numbers show that the measuring functions of money have greatly varied during the present century; further, that the public Measure of Value is at this day undergoing a most remarkable distortion. As

* 41 & 42 Victoria, cap. 49, section xix.

this distortion involves injustices of a nature similar to those that would arise from the yard unexpectedly shrinking to twenty-four inches, or the imperial gallon suddenly expanding to ten pints, should not steps be taken to correct this unlooked-for fluctuation? It is true that the preparation of a public Measure of Value presents difficulties of a nature unknown in the construction of any other standard measure; but is this a reason for neglecting the Measure of Value entirely? Ought we not rather to make some effort at least to approach that permanent stability which is everywhere recognised as the essential feature of all public measures?

The value of money varies according to the quantity in circulation compared with the amount of work to be done by it. As the tendency of populations, commerce, and civilisation is to advance, an ever increasing supply of money is required to meet the ever increasing demand arising from this tendency. If the value of money falls, the movement is a proof that more money has been utilised than advancing humanity requires. If, on the other hand, the value of money rises, the change is evidence that sufficient money has not been introduced into circulation to meet the growing requirements of mankind.

Now fluctuations in the value of money are of necessity fluctuations in the measuring function of money. When, therefore, prices generally have risen in England the alteration in values has meant that the Public Measure has shrunk, owing to more money having been introduced than was for the moment necessary for the normal advance of the people of Britain. And when prices generally have fallen, the Public Measure has expanded, owing to the supply of money not being sufficient to meet the demands arising from the advance in commerce, &c.

The supply of money, however, is a matter over which the Government can exercise considerable control. If Index Numbers show clearly that the Public Measure is steadily shrinking, what can be simpler than for Government to check the anomaly (after due notice of their intention) by closing the mints entirely to the manufacture of new money, and, if necessary, by withdrawing some of the old money from circulation. If, on the other hand, Index Numbers reveal that the Public Measure is materially expanding, every effort should be made by Government to rectify the deviation by increasing the supply of money. This might be done by reducing taxes and by issuing silver, gold, paper, or any other form of money which would serve satisfactorily in the four capacities now under consideration.

Money is the great Stimulus to Industry, and this is a function to which much attention must be paid. A judiciously applied stimulus cannot be attended with other than beneficial results; but at a certain point a stimulus ceases to operate beneficially as such, and its application beyond this point is invariably injurious. In the case of money, the stimulus to industry is so obvious that it is difficult to understand how the vast results consequent upon its operation have, to all intents and purposes, escaped the attention of the great economists of the century.* The question now is—How can this stimulus be best applied? Mankind will work for gold money, for silver money, and for paper money if this last bear the stamp of a solvent and powerful Government. It follows that a wise Legislature, with these facts before it, will stimulate the labours of the people whose destinies its guides, by the liberal issue of gold, silver, paper, or any other material which will serve effectively as money. The only danger against which it is necessary to guard is that of an over-stimulus, such as arose at the time of the South Sea Bubble or of Law's Paper Money Scheme. Fortunately the Index Numbers which it will be necessary for the State to prepare and recognise, if any intelligent control of the currency be undertaken, will show at once whether monetary stimulus be lacking or in excess. Should the

---

* Professor F. W. BAIN, in his *Principles of Wealth Creation* (1892), has vigorously protested against the errors in monetary theory arising from this and other omissions.

Index Numbers indicate a rise in prices, stimulus must be withdrawn ; should prices fall, then more stimulus must be applied until the level be restored.*

We have now to consider only the purchasing powers of money. Before the appearance of the *Wealth of Nations* it was generally believed that gold and silver were the most useful and desirable forms of wealth. And so they were. They were the great Purchasing Powers by which the monarchs of the Middle Ages maintained their positions, defended their people, or attacked those whose wealth or country they desired to possess. And notwithstanding the wide acceptance of the doctrines of the modern school of economists, money, so far from being the most "insignificant thing in the economy of society,"† is still the Great Purchasing Power, and is, consequently, still the most useful and desirable form of wealth. Money influences the world at

* "The object of a good currency is not considered by financial authorities in England to be the stimulation of industries . . . . and there are no writings that I am aware of, representing orthodox opinion on currency matters in England, in which the monetary system is discussed from this point of view."—Extract from the reply of the Secretary of the U. S. Embassy in London to an inquiry by the U. S. Legislature as to the practical effects of England's currency on the manufacturing industries of the kingdom. *Special U. S. Consular Reports, Money and Prices*, Vol. XIII. part i. p. 14. What must Americans think of England's "financial authorities" !

† J. S. MILL.

the present day just as gold and silver influenced it in centuries past. But money need no longer be made of gold and silver. In many countries the superiority of paper substitutes has been widely recognised, and those who possess these paper substitutes have the power to purchase in much the same degree as those who formerly offered gold or silver.

Experience has shown that money of silver and money of gold will command the services and commodities of mankind in practically all parts of the world. Experience has also amply proved that money of paper can be largely utilised to command the services and commodities of the more civilised peoples. Why, then, do certain statesmen of England deliberately refuse to accept a large portion of this Purchasing Power? Why do they say—The people of England shall only buy with money of gold, although other nations buy not only with gold money, but also with silver and paper money? Surely the greater the ability to buy the more will actually be bought. In a civilised society the wants of the great majority are kept in check mainly by the absence of purchasing power. Increase the amount of purchasing power any individual possesses, and he will probably proceed to gratify desires he otherwise would have been compelled to stifle. This means he will call into existence commodities which, in the absence of sufficient monetary demand, might

M

never have been produced. Thus additional
purchasing power leads to increased commerce,
and increased commerce is synonymous with
additional wealth and prosperity.

The renunciation of silver and paper purchasing power by the people of England, and the
loss of trade and wealth which this renunciation
involves, has arisen from two causes :—first, from
the difficulty of keeping paper, silver, and gold
concurrently in circulation ; and secondly, from
a misconception of the nature of money arising
from the belief that the modern device is
essentially but a "medium of exchange." The
true nature of money in all modern States is a
Right or Title to demand something from some
member or members of the State,* and this Title
can be as well expressed on paper as on pieces
of gold, silver, or copper, provided the Government are able to enforce its general recognition.
Beyond the limits of the State no such general
recognition can be enforced, and money for
external use must, therefore, be manufactured of
some valuable material which outsiders, both
civilised and uncivilised, are willing and anxious
to possess. It follows that whereas the power
of some kinds of money arises solely from its
recognition by the State, that of other kinds
results from the value the metal of which it
is made has in the eyes of those who desire to

* See in this connection Mr. DUNNING MCLEOD's *Elements
of Banking*.

obtain it. In both cases, however, the money is Power. The individual who possesses it can cause new commodities to be produced at his will, whilst the nation who wield it can create armies, fleets, or whatever may be required in the shortest possible time. Such being the case, it is evident that the more Purchasing Power the people of England control, the better for the prosperity of the British Empire. As silver and paper will buy as well as gold, let England's Purchasing Power no longer be artificially restricted to gold, but let it also include every kind of money that will command man's services. The only caution it is necessary to exercise whilst creating new Purchasing Power is to see that the supply does not exceed the demand. One important function must not be fostered to the neglect of another equally important, and consequently the State Index Number must be carefully watched, in order that when increasing the supply of Purchasing Power the Public Measure of Value is not unduly disturbed.

With regard to the difficulties that some may anticipate would arise upon the simultaneous issue of more than one kind of money, the inconveniences experienced in former ages, when both silver and gold money were concurrently unlimited legal tender, afford a valuable lesson. Had the various States of Europe not been animated by a desire to obtain each other's

monetary wealth, and had the various rulers not
rated their gold coins in a way especially
calculated to attain this object of their ambi-
tions, one half of the currency troubles of the
Middle Ages would never have existed. The
alternate disappearance now of silver, now of
gold coins, arose solely from the different legal
ratings of gold to silver simultaneously current
in the various States of Europe, and from the
impossibility of any international agreement
whereby a unity of ratio might have been
established. Before any steps could be taken
for the intelligent regulation of England's
currency, it would be necessary therefore to
come to some understanding with the principal
commercial nations of the world, in order that
the rate at which payments of silver or gold
in England would be legally recognised, might
not clash with the rate legally recognised
in other parts of the world. That such an
understanding is no longer outside the sphere of
practical politics the last Monetary Conference*
amply testifies. The issue of paper money
would not necessarily be a matter for international action. The paper money of the
Indian Empire and the laws relative to the

---

* Brussels, 1892. Austria - Hungary, Belgium, Denmark,
France, Germany, Great Britain, British India, Greece, Italy,
Mexico, The Netherlands, Norway, Portugal, Roumania,
Russia, Spain, Sweden, Switzerland, Turkey, and the United
States sent representatives to this Conference.

Greenbacks and National Bank Notes of the
United States could be studied with advantage.
There has never been any difficulty in maintaining a certain amount of inconvertible paper
money in circulation; and with the growth of
monetary knowledge and the advance of civilisation this amount would be an ever increasing
quantity.

Sufficient has now been said to show the
direction in which a just and rational control
of England's currency system should be exercised. That the Great Power which enters so
intimately into the lives of every member of the
State, and which so largely influences human
thought and action, should be made and issued
with practically no regard for its several functions, and for the parts those functions play
in the development and advancement of the
State, is an example of ignorance and neglect of
which it is impossible to find a parallel in
any other department of modern governments.
The clear intelligence of the people of England,
and their inborn love of justice and fair play,
could never have permitted such a discreditable
condition of affairs to exist had not their atten-
tions and energies been directed towards the
practical building up of their empire with such
tools as their rulers supplied to them, rather
than to a consideration of the nature and
peculiarities of the tools themselves. Now that
the superiority of these monetary instruments is

questioned, the people of Great Britain will not be long to perceive that their inability to keep pace with certain rival nations arises not from any want of energy or intelligence, but mainly from the defective and inadequate currency machinery by the aid of which they work.

CHAPTER XII.

Details to be considered in the improvement of England's monetary system—The Currency Department of State—The money of the future.

" A perfect and a just measure shalt thou have."
DEUT. xxv. 15.

THAT a legally recognised Public Measure should be liable to unexpected fluctuations is an anomaly that ought no longer to be tolerated. Not only do such fluctuations inflict most serious injustices upon large classes of the community, but, involving as they do deficiency or excess of Stimulus and variations in the strength of the Great Purchasing Power, the progress of every branch of commerce is affected, and the welfare of the whole nation disturbed. The agricultural and manufacturing classes, a portion of whose expenses are more or less fixed by custom or contract, no matter how the value of money may vary, are now suffering from a diminution in profits arising from a serious expansion in the Public Measure of Value. The banking and money-lending classes, whose welfare is inseparably bound up with that of the agricultural and manufacturing classes, are also suffering from a diminution in profits arising from the fall in rates of interest consequent upon what appears to be a plethora of money, but what is in fact a relative decrease in the demand for money—relative, when compared with the growth of the demand for money in the United States and elsewhere. The arguments already employed show that no improvement in this condition of general *malaise* can be expected so long as the supply of England's money is left to chance, and no effort whatever is made to control the Great Power. As a wide recognition of this fact will undoubtedly lead to an imperative call for monetary reform, it will be of interest to trace the lines upon which such reform should be made, in order to most benefit the people of the United Kingdom and best advance the prosperity of the British Empire.

It must be remembered that in the use and circulation of any particular kind of money, force of habit and social convention exert a very powerful influence. The great majority of the world's inhabitants have no theories, or indeed any information at all, upon the subject of money, and they are consequently guided solely by tradition and popular report. Those who have been accustomed to money of paper, generally prefer paper; those who have always handled silver, find silver money quite satisfactory; whilst those who are more familiar with gold, prefer money of this latter metal. It has always been a matter of some difficulty to induce the less informed to accept any coins or system of money which, although perhaps thoroughly sound, is not familiar to them ; and this will be the great difficulty with which the legislators of England will have to contend when the question of monetary reform receives practical consideration.

The genuine commiseration which an honest British Tar once expressed for certain French adversaries, whom he imagined to be handicapped by the (to him) queer language in which they received their orders, is somewhat in the nature of the spirit with which Englishmen of the present day are apt to regard the currency systems of foreign nations. Feelings of this kind are after all the outcome of a lack of information, and although they may do honour to the Englishman's appreciation of justice and fair play, they will hardly help him to hold his own when the weapons by aid of which he himself is fighting are not of the best that science can produce.

The first step, then, is to convince him of the defects in his own monetary tools, and at the same time to enlighten him as to the progress of those rivals who have employed tools of a different manufacture. An attempt in this direction has been made in the present work. Sir Courtenay Boyle, in summarising the conclusions which the preparation of a recent memorandum on the population, industry, and commerce of Germany, the United States, and the United Kingdom * enabled him to form, reports, "EACH COUNTRY (that is, Germany and the United States) IS FOR THE MOMENT TRAVELLING UPWARDS MORE RAPIDLY THAN WE ARE." With regard to the question of how the industrial powers of the United Kingdom can best be developed and increased, he says, "What the Government can do is to facilitate the supply of accurate and carefully collected information, and in the discharge of this duty I venture to think we are somewhat behind-hand"; an opinion which a comparison of the reports and statistics issued respectively by the Legislatures of the United Kingdom and of the United States most strongly emphasises.

But another and more practical method by which England's industrial powers can be effectively developed and increased, is to be found in the intelligent regulation of the stimulating power of money. Index Numbers must be prepared to register the level of prices generally in all parts of the kingdom, in order that fluctuations in the Public Measure of Value can be accurately gauged. Directly these Index Numbers reveal a variation of, say, 5 per cent., steps must be taken, in the manner suggested in

* Board of Trade Memorandum on the Comparative Statistics of Population, Industry, and Commerce in the United Kingdom and some Leading Foreign Countries, presented to Parliament in January, 1897.

a previous chapter, to correct the divergence, and supply or withdraw the all-important stimulus.

It is common knowledge that the value of the sovereign has considerably increased during the last twenty years. As a matter of fact the monetary yard has expanded to over fifty-one inches, and every debtor, manufacturer, and producer has been more or less affected by this iniquitous change. As a return to the old thirty-six inch monetary yard of twenty years ago might involve a repetition of injustices such as have been endured by many who are dead and gone, or who have by this time made arrangements to meet the altered condition of affairs, it will perhaps be best to commence the regulation of the currency by preventing any further distortion of the Public Measure of Value. This is a matter, however, for the people of England and of India to decide. *

Here are Mr. Sauerbeck's Index Numbers of forty-five of the principal commodities of the United Kingdom for the last five years :—

1891	.	.	72	1894	.	.	63
1892	.	.	68	1895	.	.	62
1893	.	.	68	1896	.	.	61

They show that the Public Measure of Value

* The people of India are deeply interested in this matter, for they are called upon to pay about £16,000,000 annually to the Home Government, and the recent increase in the value of gold has increased the burden by nearly 60 per cent. For each £1 of the £16,000,000 they now have to pay some sixteen rupees, where formerly about ten sufficed.

is undergoing a marked expansion. It is, therefore, the duty of the English Government to
provide sufficient additional money to correct
this movement. This can be done by the issue
of either silver or paper Purchasing Power, or✓
of both.

In matters relating to currency it is most
important that no step be taken without a notice
sufficiently long to afford to all members of the
State an opportunity to thoroughly understand
the motives, nature, and results of any proposed
legislation. As the people of England and
Ireland are not familiar with the use of paper
it will be necessary to gradually accustom them
to National Bank notes of £1 and upwards,
secured at first by reserves of gold. As they
are similarly unaccustomed to the unlimited use
of silver, and as, moreover, the extensive issue
of coins of this metal could not be successfully
carried out without an agreement by the principal nations of the world as to the relative
legal values of gold and silver, for debt-paying
purposes, an international understanding would
have to be arrived at before any steps could be
made towards the unlimited utilisation of the
less precious metal.

This, then, is the great point to be settled.
Other nations are willing to open their mints to
silver, and as silver will serve effectively as
Purchasing and Stimulating Power, there is no
reason why the people of England should not

take advantage of this Power. But there must be no unlimited coinage of all the silver that the various mine owners of the world can produce. This would mean an absence of control as unscientific and possibly as unjust as the existing absence of system. The Government must coin just as much gold and silver as may be found necessary to keep the Public Measure of Value steady, and no more.*

Because the inhabitants of the United Kingdom include the richest of the rich as well as the poorest of the poor, it is obvious that one form of money can never be convenient for all classes. Bronze coins are suitable for some; silver and bronze money for others; a grade higher in the social scale, and gold, as well as silver and bronze money, is always in circulation. Amongst the highest and wealthiest classes paper is more convenient than metal for most purposes, and but few silver and less bronze pieces are required.

And because the people of the British Empire, and those with whom the traders of the British Empire come in contact, embrace races of mankind in every degree of development, from the barbarous tribes of West Africa to the most highly civilised members of the Eastern and

---

* " The object that ought to be aimed at in a currency is to have it sufficient in quantity to cause a certain level of the average prices of the leading commodities to be maintained."— J. BARR ROBERTSON on *The Indian Currency*.

Western hemispheres, it is equally obvious that one kind of money can never suit the intelligence and wants of so diverse a multitude. The inconvertible paper currency, that would perform all the functions of money amongst the most highly cultivated and powerful societies of the West, would not prove acceptable to those who had been accustomed to consider that money ought to have some value apart from that given to it by the stamp of Government. Then again, bank notes, against which reserves of metallic money actually existed, would not satisfy the demands of those whose confidence in their Government had not been established by a long and satisfactory record of undisturbed security. A step lower and nothing but a personal retention of either gold or silver would afford that store of value and power to which those who have a just claim to money would undoubtedly be entitled; and so on.

A consideration of these facts enables us to very clearly perceive that the money of the future can never consist of paper only, as some imagine possible. Nor can it be of gold only, with a fractional token coinage. It is equally impossible to be based on silver only, or any other inferior metal. The inhabitants of the world can never arrive at one level of intelligence, power, and wealth, and consequently one kind of money will never be suitable for all classes of people and for all peoples. Vast quantities of gold, silver, and bronze money will always be required for the purchase of the minor objects of the desires of the wealthy, and also for all purposes amongst the poorer classes of mankind in every country. Endless sums of paper money will always be made use of by those the magnitude of whose operations would be inconveniently hampered by the use of metallic Purchasing and Storing Power.

This being so, the direction in which the development of England's currency system must be undertaken becomes very obvious. Money is as necessary to civilised existence as water is to human life, and to permit individual members of the State to regulate or influence the supply of either one or the other, solely for their own private ends, is no longer compatible with that condition of social development at which the people of Great Britain have now arrived. The truth of this contention is at length being recognised, and steps have been taken to help the less advanced members of the community in their efforts towards the storing of Value and Purchasing Power by the opening of Government Savings Banks. The good work should not end here, however. Government Lending Banks are if anything more necessary than Post Office Savings Banks.

The tendency towards State banking, which the establishment of a Savings Department of the British Post Office indicates, should not be restricted to an effort to assist only the poorest classes of society, but should be encouraged so as to embrace other classes. As the agricultural and manufacturing industries of the United Kingdom are now falling behind for want of stimulus, the supply of metallic money, which has for the last eighty years been restricted to gold, should be liberally augmented by a practical recognition of the utility and power of silver. This would not be so difficult as might at first seem. The merchant who carries on his business by the aid of cheques, bills, and Bank of England notes would still make use of cheques, bills, and notes, even if the "pounds sterling" that appear on the face of such paper money were really of silver as well as of gold. The fact that the banks of the United Kingdom do not keep within their coffers 5 per cent. of the gold for which they are liable, means that the millions of pounds of paper money that passes daily through the great clearing houses of the United Kingdom is within 5 per cent. of being inconvertible. If private institutions and private individuals can make use of such vast quantities of paper money which in the aggregate, and at any given moment, are all but inconvertible, how much more easily could the Government of the British Empire maintain in circulation National Bank notes against which large reserves of silver, and perhaps gold, were actually within the Treasury vaults.

The State must create a new Department, the sole duties of which must be to regulate and control every function of the Great Power. This Department must include the Royal Mint. As the vast supplies of metal brought to the mints of the United States have not been sufficient to meet the growing demands of that rapidly advancing country,* it is probable that the new Department will require all the silver and gold that may be brought to it. As these metals will only be required for monetary operations in parts of the world where ignorance of the British National Bank-note impedes its ready circulation, paper money will be the principal form in which Purchasing Power will be issued by the Currency Department. As this paper money will represent certain weights of silver or gold, it will by degrees be willingly accepted by the more advanced foreign peoples. The establishment of similar Departments for the control of the Great Power by foreign governments will lead to the establishment of international clearing houses, and eventually to international money.

Here we have a glimpse of the money of the future. The mints of the great nations will

---

* Prices generally are falling. *Vide* United States Special Consular Reports, Document 25. 54th Congress, 2nd Session (House of Representatives).

always be open to the free coinage of both gold
and silver, provided the unlimited manufacture
of such money does not disturb the measuring
functions of that already in existence. As at
present, the great majority of business transactions will be adjusted by means of paper.
But the intelligence of the people which now
accepts twelve pennies for one shilling, and
twenty shillings for one sovereign, although
neither the bronze nor the silver of which the
coins are made are worth one half of the value
of the penny or shilling, apart from the stamp
of the Mint, will, in the future, as willingly
accept paper sovereigns, against which the new
Currency Department holds gold or silver, or in
exchange for which the Government promise to
give gold or silver, as the case may be. For
obtaining the minor necessaries of life, and for
the convenience of those whose social position
does not necessitate the frequent use of cheques
or other paper money, metallic money will continue to be used. For purchasing the services or
commodities of tribes, peoples, or nations, whose
condition of civilisation and government has
not arrived at that stage when paper acknowledgments of debts are as useful as supplies of
silver or gold, the precious metals will always
be required.

The one great difference between the money
of the future and the money of the present will
be, that whereas the money of the present is

manufactured and issued without any scientific regard for its functions or influence, the money of the future will be in the hands of a special Department of Government, and will be subject to methodical and intelligent control. A continued neglect of the Great Power must of necessity lead to confusion, injustice, and retrogression, just as the neglect of any other great social force would surely imperil national welfare and affect the progress of civilisation. At the present day this neglect by the people and Government of the United Kingdom is checking and paralysing all agricultural and manufacturing enterprise. But the mischief by no means ends here. By tending to make the rich more rich, and the poor more poor, thus leading to reckless extravagance on the one hand, and to the recklessness of despair on the other, an expansion of the Public Measure of Value may bring about results of a magnitude that those who have not pondered on the influence of the Great Power little suspect. "The two greatest events in the history of mankind," says Sir Archibald Alison in his *History of Europe*, "have been directly brought about by a contraction and by an expansion of the circulating medium of society. The fall of the Roman Empire, so long ascribed in ignorance to slavery, heathenism, and moral corruption, was in reality brought about by a decline in the silver and gold mines of Spain

and Greece. And, as if Providence had intended
to reveal in the clearest manner the influence of
this mighty agent on human affairs, the resur-
rection of mankind from the ruin which those
causes had produced, was owing to a directly
opposite set of agencies being put into operation. Columbus led the way in the career of
renovation ; when he spread his sails across the
Atlantic he bore mankind and its fortunes in
his barque. The annual supply of the precious
metals for the use of the globe was tripled ;
before a century had expired the prices of
every species of produce were quadrupled.
The weight of debt and taxes insensibly wore
off under the influence of that prodigious
increase. In the renovation of industry the
relations of society were changed, the weight
of feudalism cast off, the rights of man established. Among the many concurring causes
which conspired to bring about this mighty
consummation, the most important, though
hitherto least observed, was the discovery of
Mexico and Peru. If the circulating medium
of the globe had remained stationary or
declining, as it was from 1815 to 1849, from
the effects of the South American revolution
and from English legislation, the inevitable
result must have been that it would have
become altogether inadequate to the wants of
man ; and not only would industry have been
everywhere cramped, but the price of produce

would have universally and constantly fallen.
Money would have every day become more
valuable, all other articles measured in money
less so; debt and taxes would have been
constantly increasing in weight and oppression.
The fate which crushed Rome in ancient, and
has all but crushed Great Britain in modern
times, would have been that of the whole family
of mankind. All these evils have been entirely
obviated, and the opposite set of blessings
introduced, by the opening of the great treasures
of nature in California and Australia."

The above weighty passage, which is deserving
of the widest attention, expresses only too
clearly what has occurred, and what might
occur again, owing to man's neglect to study
the workings of one of the mightiest inventions
to which he has put his hand. The supplies of
metallic money now being unearthed in South
Africa and West Australia are for the moment
in a small degree allaying the rapidity of the
fall in prices that is keeping England back; but
unless the irrational legislation which not only
closes the door to a metal that can everywhere
answer all the purposes of money, but which
further entirely omits to consider either the
influence or the functions of the Great Power,
be speedily repealed, the outlook for British
industry is far from satisfactory.

Appendix A.

33 VICT. CHAP. 10.

An Act to consolidate and amend the law relating to A.D. 1870. the Coinage and Her Majesty's Mint.

[4th April, 1870.]

[NOTE.—*This Act is printed with the substitutions in the First Schedule required by the Coinage Act, 1891 (54 & 55 Vict. c. 72), as authorised by Section 2 of that Act. The standard weight of the double florin is not given, but see Section 3 of this Act.*]

WHEREAS it is expedient to consolidate and amend the law relating to the coinage and Her Majesty's Mint:

Be it enacted by the Queen's most Excellent Majesty, by and with the advice and consent of the Lords Spiritual and Temporal, and Commons, in this present Parliament assembled, and by the authority of the same, as follows:

1. This Act may be cited as "The Coinage Act, 1870." *Short title.*

2. In this Act— *Definitions of terms.*

The term "Treasury" means the Lord High Treasurer for the time being, or the Commissioners of Her Majesty's Treasury for the time being, or any two of them;

183

The term "the Mint" means, except as expressly provided, Her Majesty's Royal Mint in England;

The term " British possession " means any colony, plantation, island, territory, or settlement within Her Majesty's dominions and not within the United Kingdom ; and

The term "person" includes a body corporate.

Standard of coins.
3. All coins made at the Mint of the denominations mentioned in the first schedule to this Act shall be of the weight and fineness specified in that schedule, and the standard trial plates shall be made accordingly.

If any coin of gold, silver, or bronze, but of any other denomination than that of the coins mentioned in the first schedule to this Act, is hereafter coined at the Mint, such coin shall be of a weight and fineness bearing the same proportion to the weight and fineness specified in that schedule as the denomination of such coin bears to the denominations mentioned in that schedule.

Provided that in the making of coins a remedy (or variation from the standard weight and fineness specified in the said first schedule) shall be allowed of an amount not exceeding the amount specified in that schedule.

Legal tender.
4. A tender of payment of money, if made in coins which have been issued by the Mint in accordance with the provisions of this Act, and have not been called in by any proclamation made in pursuance of this Act, and have not become diminished in weight, by wear or otherwise, so as to be of less weight than the current weight, that is to say, than the weight (if any) specified as the least current weight in the first schedule to this Act,

or less than such weight as may be declared by any proclamation made in pursuance of this Act, shall be a legal tender,—

    In the case of gold coins for a payment of any amount :

    In the case of silver coins for a payment of an amount not exceeding forty shillings, but for no greater amount :

    In the case of bronze coins for a payment of an amount not exceeding one shilling, but for no greater amount.

Nothing in this Act shall prevent any paper currency which under any Act or otherwise is a legal tender from being a legal tender.

5. No piece of gold, silver, copper, or bronze, or of any metal or mixed metal, of any value whatever, shall be made or issued, except by the Mint, as a coin or a token for money, or as purporting that the holder thereof is entitled to demand any value denoted thereon. Every person who acts in contravention of this section shall be liable on summary conviction to a penalty not exceeding twenty pounds. *Prohibition of other coins and tokens.*

6. Every contract, sale, payment, bill, note, instrument, and security for money, and every transaction, dealing, matter, and thing whatever relating to money, or involving the payment of or the liability to pay any money, which is made, executed, or entered into, done or had, shall be made, executed, entered into, done and had according to the coins which are current and legal tender in pursuance of this Act, and not otherwise, unless the same be made, executed, entered into, done or had according to the currency of some British possession or some foreign state. *Contracts, &c., to be made in currency.*

.

Defacing
light gold
coin.

7. Where any gold coin of the realm is below the current weight as provided by this Act, or where any coin is called in by any proclamation, every person shall, by himself or others, cut, break, or deface any such coin tendered to him in payment, and the person tendering the same shall bear the loss.

If any coin cut, broken, or defaced in pursuance of this section is not below the current weight, or has not been called in by any proclamation, the person cutting, breaking, or defacing the same shall receive the same in payment according to its denomination. Any dispute which may arise under this section may be determined by a summary proceeding.

Coining
of bullion
taken to
the Mint.

8. Where any person brings to the Mint any gold bullion, such bullion shall be assayed and coined, and delivered out to such person, without any charge for such assay or coining, or for waste in coinage.

Provided that—

(1) If the fineness of the whole of the bullion so brought to the Mint is such that it cannot be brought to the standard fineness under this Act of the coin to be coined thereout, without refining some portion of it, the master of the Mint may refuse to receive, assay, or coin such bullion:

(2) Where the bullion so brought to the Mint is finer than the standard fineness under this Act of the coin to be coined thereout, there shall be delivered to the person bringing the same such additional amount of coin as is proportionate to such superior fineness.

No undue preference shall be shown to any person under this section, and every person shall have priority according to the time at which he brought such bullion to the Mint.

9. The Treasury may from time to time issue to the master of the Mint, out of the growing produce of the Consolidated Fund, such sums as may be necessary to enable him to purchase bullion in order to provide supplies of coin for the public service. *Purchase of bullion.*

10. All sums received by the master of the Mint, or any deputy master or officer of the Mint, in payment for coin produced from bullion purchased by him, and all fees and payments received by the master or any deputy master or officer of the Mint as such, shall (save as otherwise provided in the case of any branch mint in a British possession by a proclamation respecting such branch mint) be paid into the receipt of the Exchequer, and carried to the Consolidated Fund. *Payment of profits, &c., to Exchequer.*

11. It shall be lawful for Her Majesty, with the advice of Her Privy Council, from time to time by proclamation to do all or any of the following things ; namely, *Regulations by proclamation.*

(1) To determine the dimension of and design for any coin :

(2) To determine. the denominations of coins to be coined at the Mint :

(3) To diminish the amount of remedy allowed by the first schedule to this Act in the case of any coin :

(4) To determine the weight (not being less than the weight (if any) specified in the first schedule to this Act) below which a coin, whether diminished in weight by wear or otherwise, is not to be a current or a legal tender :

(5) To call in coins of any date or denomination, or any coins coined before the date in the proclamation mentioned :

(6) To direct that any coins, other than gold, silver, or bronze, shall be current and be a legal tender for the payment of any amount not exceeding the amount specified in the proclamation, and not exceeding five shillings :

(7) To direct that coins coined in any foreign country shall be current, and be a legal tender, at such rates, up to such amounts, and in such portion of Her Majesty's dominions as may be specified in the proclamation ; due regard being had in fixing those rates to the weight and fineness of such coins, as compared with the current coins of this realm :

(8) To direct the establishment of any branch of the Mint in any British possession, and impose a charge for the coinage of gold thereat ; determine the application of such charge ; and determine the extent to which such branch is to be deemed part of the Mint, and to which coins issued therefrom are to be current and be a legal tender, and to be deemed to be issued from the Mint :

(9) To direct that the whole or any part of this Act shall apply to and be in force in any British possession, with or without any modifications contained in the proclamation :

(10) To regulate any matters relative to the coinage and the Mint within the present prerogative of the Crown which are not provided for by this Act :

(11) To revoke or alter any proclamation previously made.

Every such proclamation shall come into operation
on the date therein in that behalf mentioned, and
shall have effect as if it were enacted in this Act.

12. For the purpose of ascertaining that coins *Trial of the*
issued from the Mint have been coined in accordance *pyx.*
with this Act, a trial of the pyx shall be held at least
once in every year in which coins have been issued
from the Mint.

It shall be lawful for Her Majesty, with the advice
of Her Privy Council, from time to time, by order, to
make regulations respecting the trial of the pyx and
all matters incidental thereto, and in particular respecting the following matters ; viz.,

(1) The time and place of the trial :
(2) The setting apart out of the coins issued by the
Mint certain coins for the trial :
(3) The summoning of a jury of not less than six
out of competent freemen of the mystery
of goldsmiths of the city of London or other
competent persons.
(4) The attendance at the trial of the jury so
summoned, and of the proper officers of
the Treasury, the Board of Trade, and the
Mint, and the production of the coins so
set apart, and of the standard trial plates ·
and standard weights :
(5) The proceedings at and conduct of the trial,
including the nomination of some person to
preside thereat, and the swearing of the
jury, and the mode of examining the coins :
(6) The recording and the publication of the
verdict, and the custody of the record

thereof, and the proceedings (if any) to be taken in consequence of such verdict.

Every such order shall come into operation on the date therein in that behalf mentioned, and shall have effect as if it were enacted in this Act, but may be revoked or altered by any subsequent order under this section.

Regulations by Treasury. 13. The Treasury may from time to time do all or any of the following things :

(1) Fix the number and duties of the officers of and persons employed in the Mint :

(2) Make regulations and give directions (subject to the provisions of this Act and any proclamation made thereunder) respecting the general management of the Mint, and revoke and alter such regulations and directions.

Master and Officers of Mint.

Master of Mint. 14. The Chancellor of the Exchequer for the time being shall be the master, worker, and warden of Her Majesty's Royal Mint in England, and governor of the Mint in Scotland.

Provided that nothing in this section shall render the Chancellor of the Exchequer incapable of being elected to or of sitting or voting in the House of Commons, or vacate the seat of the person who at the passing of this Act holds the office of Chancellor of the Exchequer.

All duties, powers, and authorities imposed on or vested in or to be transacted before the master of the Mint may be performed and exercised by or transacted before him or his sufficient deputy.

Deputy masters and officers. 15. The Treasury may from time to time appoint deputy masters and other officers and persons for the purpose of carrying on the business of the Mint in the United Kingdom or elsewhere, and assign them their duties and award them their salaries.

The master of the Mint may from time to time promote, suspend, and remove any such deputy masters, officers, and persons.

Standard Trial Plates and Weights.

16. The standard trial plates of gold and silver used for determining the justness of the gold and silver coins of the realm issued from the Mint, which now exist or may hereafter be made, and all books, documents, and things used in connexion therewith or in relation thereto, shall be in the custody of the Board of Trade, and shall be kept in such places and in such manner as the Board of Trade may from time to time direct; and the performance of all duties in relation to such trial plates shall be part of the business of the Standard weights and measures Department of the Board of Trade. *Custody, &c., of standard trial plates.*

The Board of Trade shall from time to time, when necessary, cause new standard trial plates to be made and duly verified, of such standard fineness as may be in conformity with the provisions of this Act.

17. The standard weights for weighing and testing the coin of the realm shall be placed in the custody of the Board of Trade, and be kept in such places and in such manner as the Board of Trade may from time to time direct; and the performance of all duties in relation to such standard weights shall be part of the business of the Standard weights and measures Department of the Board of Trade. *Standard weights for coin.*

The Board of Trade shall from time to time cause weights of each coin of the realm for the time being, and of multiples of such of those weights as may be required, to be made and duly verified; and those weights, when approved by Her Majesty in Council, shall be the standard weights for determining the justness of the weight of and for weighing such coin.

The master of the Mint shall from time to time cause copies to be made of such standard weights, and once at least in every year the Board of Trade and the master of the Mint shall cause such copies to be compared and duly verified with the standard weights in the custody of the Board of Trade.

All weights which are not less in weight than the weight prescribed by the first schedule to this Act for the lightest coin, and are used for weighing coin, shall be compared with the said standard weights, and if found to be just shall, on payment of such fee, not exceeding five shillings, as the Board of Trade from time to time prescribe, be marked by some officer of the Standard weights and measures Department of the Board of Trade with a mark approved of by the Board of Trade, and notified in the *London Gazette;* and a weight which is required by this section to be so compared, and is not so marked, shall not be deemed a just weight for determining the weight of gold and silver coin of the realm.

If any person forges or counterfeits such mark, or any weight so marked, or wilfully increases or diminishes any weight so marked, or knowingly utters, sells, or uses any weight with such counterfeit mark, or any weight so increased or diminished, or knowingly uses any weight declared by this section not to be a just weight, such person shall be liable to a penalty not exceeding fifty pounds.

All fees paid under this section shall be paid into the Exchequer, and carried to the Consolidated Fund.

Legal Proceedings.

18. Any summary proceeding under this Act may Summary procedure.
be taken, and any penalty under this Act may be
recovered,—

In England, before two justices of the peace in
manner directed by the Act of the session of the
eleventh and twelfth years of the reign of Her present
Majesty, chapter forty-three, intituled " An Act to
"facilitate the performance of the duties of justices
"of the peace out of sessions within England and
" Wales with respect to summary convictions and
" orders," and any Act amending the same.

In Scotland, in manner directed by The Summary
Procedure Act, 1864.

In Ireland, so far as respects Dublin, in manner
directed by the Acts regulating the powers of justices
of the peace or the police of Dublin Metropolis, and
elsewhere in manner directed by The Petty Sessions
(Ireland) Act, 1851, and any Act amending the same.

In any British possession, in the courts, and before
such justices or magistrates, and in the manner in
which the like proceedings and penalties may be
taken and recovered by the law of such possession,
or as near thereto as circumstances admit, or in
such other courts, or before such other justices or
magistrates, or in such other manner as any Act
or Ordinance having the force of law in such
possession may from time to time provide.

Miscellaneous.

19. This Act, save as expressly provided by this Extent of Act.
Act, or by any proclamation made thereunder, shall
not extend to any British possession.

O

20. The Acts mentioned in the first part of the
second schedule to this Act are hereby repealed to
the extent in the third column of such schedule
mentioned, and those mentioned in the second part
of the same schedule are hereby repealed entirely.

Provided that,—

(1) This repeal shall not affect anything already
done or suffered, or any right already
acquired or accrued :

(2) All weights for weighing coin which have
before the passing of this Act been marked
at the Mint or by any proper officer shall be
deemed to have been marked under this Act :

(3) Every branch of the Mint which at the
passing of this Act issues coins in any
British possession shall, until the date fixed
by any proclamation made in pursuance of
this Act with respect to such branch Mint,
continue in all respects to have the same
power of issuing coins and be in the same
position as if this Act had not passed, and
coins so issued shall be deemed for the
purpose of this Act to have been issued
from the Mint :

(4) The said Acts (unless relating to a branch
Mint and unless in the said schedule
expressly otherwise mentioned) are not
repealed so far as they apply to any British
possession to which this Act does not
extend until a proclamation directing that
this Act or any part thereof, with or without any modification contained in the
proclamation, shall be in force in such
British possession comes into operation.

FIRST SCHEDULE.

Denomination of Coin.	Standard Weight. Imperial Weight. Grains.	Standard Weight. Metric Weight. Grams.	Least Current Weight. Imperial Weight. Grains.	Least Current Weight. Metric Weight. Grams.	Standard Fineness.	Remedy Allowance. Weight per Piece. Imperial Grains.	Remedy Allowance. Weight per Piece. Metric Grams.	Remedy Allowance. Millesimal Fineness.
GOLD:								
Five Pound	616·37239	39·94028	612·50000	39·68935	Eleven-twelfths fine gold, one-twelfth alloy; or millesimal fineness 916·6.	1·00	0·06479	2
Two Pound	246·54895	15·97611	245·00000	15·87574		0·40	0·02592	
Sovereign	123·27447	7·98805	122·50000	7·93787		0·20	0·01296	
Half Sovereign	61·63723	3·99402	61·12500	3·96893		0·15	0·00972	
SILVER:								
Crown	436·36363	28·2759	—	—	Thirty-seven fortieths fine silver, three-fortieths alloy; or millesimal fineness 925.	2·000	0·1296	4
Double Florin	—	—	—	—		1·678	0·1087	
Half Crown	218·18181	14·13795	—	—		1·264	0·0788	
Florin	174·54545	11·31036	—	—		0·997	0·0646	
Shilling	87·27272	5·65518	—	—		0·578	0·0375	
Sixpence	43·63636	2·82759	—	—		0·346	0·0224	
Groat or Fourpence	29·09090	1·88506	—	—		0·262	0·0170	
Threepence	21·81818	1·41379	—	—		0·212	0·0138	
Twopence	14·54545	0·94853	—	—		0·144	0·0093	
Penny	7·27272	0·47126	—	—		0·087	0·0056	
BRONZE:								
Penny	145·83333	9·44984	—	—	Mixed metal, copper, tin and zinc.	2·91666	0·18899	None.
Halfpenny	87·50000	5·66990	—	—		1·75000	0·11339	
Farthing	43·75000	2·83495	—	—		0·87500	0·05669	

The weight and fineness of the coins specified in this Schedule are according to what is provided by the Act fifty-six George the Third, chapter sixty-eight, that the gold coin of the United Kingdom of Great Britain and Ireland should hold such weight and fineness as were prescribed in the then existing Mint indenture (that is to say), that there should be nine hundred and thirty-four sovereigns and one ten shilling piece contained in twenty pounds weight troy of standard gold, of the fineness at the trial of the same of twenty-two carats fine gold and two carats of alloy in the pound weight troy ; and further, as regards silver coin, that there should be sixty-six shillings in every pound troy of standard silver of the fineness of eleven ounces two pennyweights of fine silver and eighteen pennyweights of alloy in every pound weight troy.

SECOND SCHEDULE.

FIRST PART.

Acts partly repealed.

Year and Chapter.	Title.	Extent of Repeal.
2 Hen. 6. c. 17 *	For regulating and ascertaining the fineness of silver work.	So much as relates to the master of the Mint.
29 & 30 Vict. c. 82 . .	An Act to amend the Acts relating to the standard weights and measures, and to the standard trial pieces of the coin of the realm.	Section thirteen.

* c. 14. in Ruffhead.

SECOND PART.

Acts wholly repealed.

Year and Chapter.	Title.
18 & 19 Cha. 2. c. 5*	An Act for encouraging of coinage.
‡ 6 Anne, c. 57 † .	An Act for ascertaining the rates of foreign coins in Her Majesty's plantations in America.
‡ 13 Geo. 3. c. 57 .	An Act to explain and amend an Act made in the fourth year of His present Majesty, intituled "An Act to prevent "paper bills of credit hereafter to be "issued in any of His Majesty's "colonies or plantations in America "from being declared to be a legal "tender in payments of money, and "to prevent the legal tender of such "bills as are now subsisting from "being prolonged beyond the periods "limited for calling in and sinking the "same."
14 Geo. 3. c. 73 .	An Act for applying a certain sum of money for calling in and recoining the deficient gold coin of this realm; and for regulating the manner of receiving the same at the Bank of England, and of taking there an account of the deficiency of the said coin and making satisfaction for the same; and for authorizing all persons to cut and deface all gold coin that shall not be allowed to be current by His Majesty's proclamation.
14 Geo. 3. c. 92 .	An Act for regulating and ascertaining the weights to be made use of in weighing the gold and silver coin of this kingdom.

* 18 Cha. 2. in Ruffhead. † c. 30. in Ruffhead.
‡ Repealed as to the whole of Her Majesty's dominions upon the passing of this Act.

Year and Chapter.	Title.
15 Geo. 3. c. 30 .	An Act for allowing the officer appointed to mark or stamp the weights to be made use of in weighing the gold and silver coin of this kingdom, in pursuance of an Act made in the last session of Parliament, to take certain fees in the execution of his office.
39 Geo. 3. c. 94 .	An Act to ascertain the salary of the master and worker of His Majesty's Mint.
52 Geo. 3. c. 138 .	An Act for the further prevention of the counterfeiting of silver tokens issued by the Governor and Company of the Bank of England called dollars, and of silver pieces issued and circulated by the said Governor and Company called tokens, and for the further prevention of frauds practised by the imitation of the notes or bills of the said Governor and Company.
52 Geo. 3. c. 157 .	An Act to prevent the issuing and circulating of pieces of gold and silver or other metal, usually called tokens, except such as are issued by the Banks of England and Ireland respectively.
54 Geo. 3. c. 4 .	An Act to continue until six weeks after the commencement of the next session of Parliament an Act passed in the last session of Parliament, intituled "An "Act to continue and amend an Act of "the present session, to prevent the "issuing and circulating of pieces of "gold and silver or other metal, usually "called tokens, except such as are "issued by the Banks of England and "Ireland respectively."
56 Geo. 3. c. 68 .	An Act to provide for a new silver coinage, and to regulate the currency of the gold and silver coin of this realm.
57 Geo. 3. c. 46 .	An Act to prevent the issuing and circulating of pieces of copper or other metal usually called tokens.

Year and Chapter.	Title.
57 Geo. 3. c. 67 .	An Act to regulate certain offices, and abolish others, in His Majesty's Mints in England and Scotland respectively.
57 Geo. 3. c. 113 .	An Act to prevent the further circulation of dollars and tokens issued by the Governor and Company of the Bank of England for the convenience of the public.
6 Geo. 4. c. 79 .	An Act to provide for the assimilation of the currency and monies of account throughout the United Kingdom of Great Britain and Ireland.
6 Geo. 4. c. 98 .	An Act to prevent the further circulation of tokens issued by the Governor and Company of the Bank of Ireland for the convenience of the public, and for defraying the expense of exchanging such tokens.
1 & 2 Will. 4. c. 10	An Act to reduce the salary of the master and worker of His Majesty's Mint.
7 Will. 4. & 1 Vict. c. 9 . .	An Act to amend several Acts relating to the Royal Mint.
12 & 13 Vict. c. 41.	An Act to extend an Act of the fifty-sixth year of King George the Third, for providing for a new silver coinage, and for regulating the currency of the gold and silver coin of this realm.
22 & 23 Vict. c. 30.	An Act to extend the enactments relating to the copper coin to coin of mixed metal.
26 & 27 Vict. c. 74.	An Act to enable Her Majesty to declare gold coins to be issued from Her Majesty's Branch Mint at Sydney, New South Wales, a legal tender for payments; and for other purposes relating thereto.
29 & 30 Vict c. 65.	An Act to enable Her Majesty to declare gold coins to be issued from Her Majesty's Colonial Branch Mints a legal tender for payments; and for other purposes relating thereto.

APPENDIX B.

52 & 53 VICT. CHAP. 58.

A.D. 1889. An Act to amend the Coinage Act, 1870, as respects Light Gold Coins.   [30th August, 1889.]

33 & 34 Vict. c. 10.

WHEREAS by Section 7 of the Coinage Act, 1870, it is enacted as follows:

"Where any gold coin of the realm is below the "current weight as provided by this Act, or where "any coin is called in by any proclamation, every "person shall by himself or others, cut, break, or "deface any such coin tendered to him in payment, "and the person tendering the same shall bear the "loss":

And whereas the said section has failed to maintain the integrity of the gold coinage of the realm, and it is expedient to provide for the exchange of a portion of such gold coins as, owing to fair wear and tear, are below the least current weight without charging the holders thereof for the loss:

Be it therefore enacted by the Queen's most Excellent Majesty, by and with the advice and consent of the Lords Spiritual and Temporal, and Commons, in this present Parliament assembled, and by the authority of the same, as follows:

200

1.—(1) Any gold coin of the realm coined before the reign of Her present Majesty which is below the least current weight as provided by the Coinage Act, 1870, may, within the time and in the manner from time to time directed by Her Majesty the Queen in Council, be tendered for exchange, and, if it has not been illegally dealt with, shall (notwithstanding any-thing in Section 7 of the Coinage Act, 1870) be exchanged or paid for by or on behalf of the Mint at its nominal value : *Provision as to exchange of light pre-Victorian gold coins.*

(2) Any expenses incurred by reason of such exchange or payment shall be defrayed out of moneys provided by Parliament.

(3) For the purposes of this Act a gold coin shall be deemed to have been illegally dealt with, where the coin has been impaired, diminished, or lightened otherwise than by fair wear and tear, or has been defaced by having any name, word, device, or number stamped thereon, whether the coin has or has not been thereby diminished or lightened :

(4) In a gold coin loss of weight exceeding the amount specified in that behalf in the schedule to this Act shall for the purposes of this Act be *prima facie* evidence that the coin has been impaired, diminished, or lightened otherwise than by fair wear and tear.

2. This Act may be cited as the Coinage Act, 1889. *Short titles.*

This Act and the Coinage Act, 1870, may be cited together as the Coinage Acts, 1870 and 1889

SCHEDULE.

Loss of WEIGHT which is to be evidence of COIN being illegally dealt with.

Description of Gold Coin.	Amount of Loss of Weight in each coin which is to be evidence that the coin has been illegally dealt with.
A sovereign or half-sovereign coined before the reign of Her present Majesty.	Loss exceeding four grains from the standard weight.

Note.—In the case of any coin of higher denomination than a sovereign, a loss on each coin, proportionate to that on the sovereign, shall be evidence that the coin has been illegally dealt with. The standard weight of a sovereign is 123˙27447 grains, and the standard weight of a half-sovereign is 61˙63723 grains.

APPENDIX C.

54 & 55 VICT. CHAP. 72.

An Act to amend the Coinage Act, 1870. A.D. 1891.

[5th August, 1891.]

BE it enacted by the Queen's most Excellent Majesty, by and with the advice and consent of the Lords Spiritual and Temporal, and Commons, in this present Parliament assembled, and by the authority of the same, as follows :

1.—(1) It shall be lawful for Her Majesty, by Order in Council, to direct that gold coins of the realm which have not been called in by proclamation and are below the least current weight as provided by the Coinage Act, 1870, shall, if they have not been illegally dealt with, and subject to such conditions as to time, manner, and order of presentation, as may be mentioned in the Order, be exchanged or paid for by or on behalf of the Mint at their nominal value. *(Provision as to exchange of light gold coins.)* *(33 & 34 Vict. c. 10.)*

(2) For the purposes of this Act a gold coin shall be deemed to have been illegally dealt with where the coin has been impaired, diminished, or lightened otherwise than by fair wear and tear, or has been defaced by having any name, word, device, or number

203

stamped thereon, whether the coin has or has not been thereby diminished or lightened.

(3) In a sovereign or half sovereign loss of weight exceeding three grains from the standard weight shall, for the purposes of this Act, be *prima facie* evidence that the coin has been impaired, diminished, or lightened otherwise than by fair wear and tear.

(4) Towards meeting the expenses to be incurred in pursuance of this section the sum of four hundred thousand pounds shall be charged on and issued from the Consolidated Fund in the year ending the thirty-first day of March, one thousand eight hundred and ninety-two, and, so far as not immediately required, may be invested in such manner as the Treasury direct; and any interest thereon shall be applied for the purposes of this section.

Remedy allowances for coin.

2. The remedy allowances for gold, silver, and bronze coins shall be such as are specified in the schedule to this Act; and in all copies of the Coinage Act, 1870, printed after the passing of this Act, the First Schedule to that Act shall be printed so as to give effect to the amendments made by this section.

Short titles and construction.

3.—(1) This Act may be cited as the Coinage Act, 1891.

(2) This Act and the Coinage Act, 1870, may be cited together as the Coinage Acts, 1870 and 1891.

(3) Expressions used in this Act have the same meaning as in the Coinage Act, 1870.

SCHEDULE.

Denomination of Coin.	Standard Fineness.	Remedy Allowance.		Millesimal Fineness.
		Weight per Piece.		
		Imperial Grains.	Metric Grams.	
GOLD:	Eleven - twelfths fine gold, one-twelfth alloy; or millesimal fineness 916·6.			
Five-pound . .		1·00	0·L6479	
Two-pound . .		0·40	0·02592	2
Sovereign . .		0·20	0·01296	
Half-sovereign .		0·15	0·00972	
SILVER:	Thirty-seven for-tieths fine silver, three - fortieths alloy; or millesimal fineness 925.			
Crown . .		2·000	0·1296	
Double-florin .		1·678	0·1087	
Half-crown . .		1·264	0·0788	
Florin . .		0·997	0·0646	
Shilling . .		0·578	0·0375	
Sixpence . .		0·346	0·0224	4
Groat or Fourpence		0·262	0·0170	
Threepence . .		0·212	0·0138	
Twopence . .		0·144	0·0093	
Penny . .		0·087	0·0056	
BRONZE:	Mixed metal, copper, tin, and zinc.			
Penny . .		2·91666	0·18899	
Halfpenny . .		1·75000	0·11339	None.
Farthing . .		0·87500	0·05669	

www.ingramcontent.com/pod-product-compliance
Lightning Source LLC
Chambersburg PA
CBHW030327270326
41926CB00010B/1538